To Ta

[barcode] GW01072140

[signature]

THE
MOTHER
OF ALL
NETWORKS

THE
MOTHER
OF ALL
NETWORKS

Britain and the Commonwealth
in the 21st Century

David Howell
with a foreword by William Hague

GILGAMESH

The Mother of all Networks,
Britain and the Commonwealth
in the 21st Century

Published by Gilgamesh Publishing in 2018
Email: info@gilgamesh-publishing.co.uk
www.gilgamesh-publishing.co.uk

ISBN 978-1-908531-94-0

CIP Data: A catalogue for this book is
available from the British Library

CONTENTS

Foreword by William Hague
    The Rt. Hon. Lord Hague of Richmond   7
Author's Preface   9
Introduction   13
Chapter One: Networks, The Microchip &
    The Conditions of the 21st Century   21
Chapter Two: The UK's Foreign Policy &
    The Need for Change   43
Chapter Three: Our Real Friends   59
Chapter Four: Twenty Years of Disappointment   81
Chapter Five: Towards a Commonwealth
    Mark Two   101
Chapter Six: The Next Step: A Fresh Foreign
    Policy for Britain   125
APPENDIX   House of Commons Foreign
    Affairs Committee   139

FOREWORD

by William Hague
The Rt. Hon. Lord Hague of Richmond.

As a minister, campaigner and parliamentarian, David Howell has for the last two decades been the foremost advocate of the renewal and reinvigoration of the Commonwealth. With persistence and foresight he has consistently argued that Britain can only gain from making more of its myriad personal, commercial, linguistic and cultural links with fully a quarter of all the nations on earth.

In 1996 he was the prime author of a House of Commons report calling on the British Government to improve relations with its Commonwealth partners. In the Coalition Government formed in 2010 he was a persuasive force for doing so in practice. As I set out to put new energy into our bilateral links with many Commonwealth countries as Foreign Secretary, I often had his words and arguments in my mind.

The central insight of this argument has always been that the twenty first century is bringing a world of networks rather than blocs, and that a network that happens already to encompass nearly a third of the world's population will be of increased relevance and hold immense new opportunities. Commonwealth nations represent a steadily increasing proportion of the world's people and the trade between them. With sixty per cent of their people under the age of 30, they are 'in many ways the face of the future', as Her Majesty the Queen has said.

David Howell has always been clear that the Commonwealth is not a substitute for the European Union. But as we prepare to leave the EU, it is right to examine the strengthening of our ties with parts of the world who thought we had turned away from them. They, like Britain, can benefit greatly from expanding their ties in education, legal systems, trade and the reinforcement of shared democratic values. As India and other Asian nations gain in economic and political weight, it would be a serious oversight not to make the most of such vital connections.

With London hosting the Commonwealth Heads of Government in 2018, this book can help all concerned think about what to make of this extraordinary organisation in the future. It contains a vision and a plan wholly oriented to the future – one which leaders and policy makers might disagree with but they should most definitely not ignore.

William Hague
The Rt. Hon. Lord Hague of Richmond.
February 2018

AUTHOR'S PREFACE

'*But, it will inevitably be asked, how can such a disparate and scattered grouping possibly be a force and a weight in these dangerous and contentious times? Who will take the lead? It can never be a trade bloc. Where is central control going to be?*

To understand the answer to these questions requires the biggest shift of all between the 20th century and the 21st century mindset, a shift which many still find it impossible to make.

In the 20th Century the solution had to be in terms of blocs, consolidated organisations, centrally controlled in the name of efficiency, organisational pyramids, perhaps with some delegation, but basically radiating down from a superior and central point.

All this has now been invalidated, not only in business but in governmental affairs and in relations between countries and societies. Thanks to the extraordinary power and pervasiveness of the information revolution we live in an era now not of blocs and pyramid tiers of power and management but of networks and meshes, both formal and informal. By accident as much as design the Commonwealth emerges from a controversial past to take a perfect place in this new order of thinking and acting.'

(Extract from a speech to the Royal Commonwealth Society, 25 Northumberland Avenue. 17th of May 2001)

****

This is a story of an idea awakening from slumber. It is an account, from one personal viewpoint and drawing on a series of speeches, lectures, published articles, books, letters, notes and memoranda over two decades – of failure, failure, failure, and then at last some glimmerings of success.

There is no final triumphant moment, no completion, just the discovery, after years of banging heads against a brick wall, that the wall has a gateway. The ice of total disinterest, especially in Whitehall, Westminster and the media generally, has at last began to melt and the first spring streams of interest, support and recommitment are beginning to flow.

I am talking about the enormous Commonwealth network which spreads across half the earth's landmass and just under one third of humankind, about its total transformation to something almost entirely new and about evolving British attitudes towards it.

Once long ago, in the post war years of the last century, the Commonwealth was a major British concern, the centre of thinking about Britain's future position in the world.

Then the concern faded, was marginalised, almost forgotten. Now, decades later, and for reasons which in some quarters are still not fully grasped, interest and concern are returning at the very heart of the British government. It is truly a case of Commonwealth Redux.

One further word of warning - it may not work. The great new markets and the smaller nations of the Commonwealth maybe not that interested when Britain comes back to them. After all Britain has been away a long time. Both its visa arrangements and its policy towards students from Commonwealth countries remain unwelcoming. Much will depend on acquiring the habit of treating giant India (half the Commonwealth) with the profound respect it merits. New relationships will have to be carefully forged and old scores carefully buried.

The reader should be reminded that many of the texts which follow were written or spoken decades ago. Some of them will seem oddly out of date. What they provide is an unfolding story rather than an up-to-the-minute picture of a world in flux. There is some repetition, even contradiction. Events change. Views evolve. Understanding is requested.

David Howell
Lord Howell of Guildford
March 2018

INTRODUCTION

On November 22nd, 1995 the Foreign Affairs Committee of the House of Commons at Westminster issued a report. The report contained a revolutionary message. The message was that the Commonwealth, far from being a redundant organisation (a spent force and a leftover from imperial glories), was transforming itself into a modern network of enormous potential, both economic and political.

The report concluded that "the Commonwealth is acquiring a new significance in a rapidly emerging world". Policymakers, it urged, should bring this major change to the forefront of their thinking.

From the UK point of view, it argued that this offered new opportunities which should be recognised and seized, and indeed exploited with vigour and imagination.

The view that Commonwealth relations had become the Cinderella in the shaping of British foreign policy and the promotion of British interests, although refuted by ministers who appeared as witness to the inquiry, seemed all too clear to the Committee. The report urged a stronger emphasis on the Commonwealth dimension right across the government as a whole.

The message went nowhere. A tepid response came from the government, some six months later, assuring the Committee that Ministers would 'discuss the priorities', that they were 'conscious of the advantages which the Commonwealth links could bestow on British companies and institutions, and would examine how these links 'could be used to best effect.

But that was it. The rest was silence. Hardly any of the recommendations from the committee were put into effect. Within the Whitehall hierarchy the Commonwealth remained a fractional part of its concerns. The Commonwealth Office had long since vanished, as had the post of Commonwealth Secretary. Inside the Foreign & Commonwealth Office a handful of officials were still struggling bravely to keep the issue alive at all, barely succeeding. Indeed, within a few years, trendy voices in the Foreign Office would be actually arguing that the name of the department should be changed and the word Commonwealth dropped forever from its title. Fortunately, they were frustrated.

Soon after the report the government changed and the preoccupations of the new administration turned elsewhere. Some speeches about the Commonwealth were made by the Labour government's eloquent new Foreign Secretary, Robin Cook, but he was almost alone in Government. Little or no action followed. Minds were elsewhere as New Labour discovered its newfound interest in the European Union and addressed European issues with the zeal of converts. In effect the Commonwealth sank from sight, or at least from the sight of policy-makers, opinion-formers and the Westminster world.

From one source almost alone came the steady reminder that the modern Commonwealth was a hidden asset. That source was H.M. The Queen and members of her family. While Ministers in successive governments looked the other way her insistence, in line with her very first vows as monarch, was that it would prove to be the face of the future, not the past.

Today the situation has changed beyond recognition. In place of a lonely group within the Foreign and Commonwealth Office there is now a lively Cabinet Office Unit focussing entirely on the issues and preparations for a major Commonwealth Summit, or Heads of Government meeting, to be held in London in April 2018. Between 60 and 80 officials now work where six struggled before. For the first time in history both Buckingham Palace and Windsor Castle are opening doors for conference activities. Meetings of Commonwealth Trade Ministers have been revived. Commonwealth Education Ministers meet regularly and generate new ideas. After more than twenty years the Commonwealth is beginning to be viewed from London, and across the nation, as it was urged to be in vain all that time ago. The contrast between the nineteen-nineties and today could hardly be greater.

How has this extraordinary, if very belated, change come about? For some, it is the culmination of years of persistent argument, advanced through many channels to a hitherto largely disinterested media, that a great opportunity was being missed. For others the trigger has been the British decision to leave the EU. Without a doubt this has led to a sharp revival of Whitehall interest in wider global networks of which the Commonwealth is undoubtedly one, possibly the biggest.

But in truth the build-up to the new mindset has been taking shape spasmodically over many years, driven by a number of forces bigger than any government.

Down the years a case has grown for a fundamental change in Britain's foreign policy strategy and in the way Britain views itself in a rapidly changing world landscape. Long before Brexit, it had become increasingly clear that for Britain to see its main destiny as lying within Europe was simply no longer enough in the new conditions of the 21st century.

The staggering expansion of communications technology, the rise of Asia and the extraordinary changes in the past two decades brought about by what has been labelled the fourth industrial revolution, or the second wave of globalisation, were all conspiring long before Brexit to impel Britain to rethink its world position.

One other seemingly pure chance was the decision made at the Commonwealth heads of government meeting in Malta in November 2015, to locate the next heads of government conference in London early in 2018, at which point Britain would take over the chairmanship of the Commonwealth itself, previously held by Malta and before that by Sri Lanka.

The decision at Malta that Britain should be the next Commonwealth Heads of Government host had nothing at all to do with Brexit and was made at a time when few people foresaw the Brexit decision as at all likely. How it came about is not clear, although there were certainly some articulate voices urging this course. Perhaps it should be put down to pure chance. The original idea had been to hold it in Vanuatu but a cruel and devastating typhoon put paid to that. Indeed, that the Commonwealth leaders were meeting at Malta in the first place, rather than Mauritius as earlier intended, was due to a chance conversation in an aeroplane. The tumble of events and their outcome provide a classic example of the way in which factors can coincide by chance, and in doing so alter the pattern of history.

The Commonwealth connection is by no means the only answer to Britain's post-Brexit role in the world. At the risk of repetition we now live in a world of expanding networks driven by algorithms of unimaginable power and influence, and the Commonwealth is only one network amongst them, large, admittedly not strong in every sinew and very widely misunderstood. Its potential derives not from any central authority or government strategy but from almost the opposite - namely that power now lies increasingly with the crowd, with the grass roots and with the myriad impulses of markets, interests, professions, civil society groups of almost every kind and individuals, as well as with cities as much as states.

This is an entirely different world, a web rather than a diplomatic chessboard, and it just happens, by nobody's plan, that the Commonwealth structure has evolved in a manner uniquely suited to it and is continuing to do so.

Every prejudice will find a little on which to feed in the Commonwealth story. Those who look back and see much good in the old British Empire clash with those at the other extreme who see only a legacy of colonialism and oppression. Some see in it a secret plot to frustrate EU integration, when it is nothing of the kind, an organization of an entirely different nature. Some sneer at it as pure nostalgia, without seeing that everything has a changed. One misguided official even tried to label the new interest as Empire 2.0.

Across the Commonwealth monarchists vie with republicans, historians with historicists, old Commonwealth hands blind to its obvious faults line up against hostile columnists blind to its potential. And all the while the media hovers, looking only for a punch-up, a scandal somewhere, a deviation, a nastiness on which to swoop. All who survey an association covering a third of the world's population are bound to find something, somewhere to satisfy their viewpoint. But when all is said and done the message here is that the forces which are now pulling the Commonwealth together are getting stronger, much stronger, than the forces and voices pulling it apart.

The title of this book, The Mother of All Networks, seeks to capture what the Commonwealth, so long shunned, ignored and downgraded in the list of British interests, is about to become.

This is the body the strengthening of which the UK should now make its key foreign policy priority and together with which it should re-build its own foreign policy priorities. It should do so because this route offers far the best way both for a nation such as the UK, with its history and mix of experience and skills, to make a maximum contribution to meeting the world's many ills.

In particular the UK should consider transferring the administration of that part of its overseas development effort which at present goes through the EU from that unhappy channel to the Commonwealth system and encourage both other Commonwealth members to do likewise and the Secretariat to develop the full capacity to handle this role. The current bias in EU programmes towards the Francophonie states could thereby be usefully corrected.

This single move would give the Commonwealth huge new prestige and resources, as well as directing aid efforts far more effectively to poorer Commonwealth member states, to whom the richer countries owe the strongest duty.

So when the British Prime Minister calls for children to be taught a 'greater sense of British identity', that should read 'British and Commonwealth identity'. That alone conveys the broader and outward-looking sense of interdependence and duty which is the true message with which young British children should carry in today's world.

Of course, the UK must continue to be the best possible local member of our European region in which geography places it – as, incidentally it nearly always has been, shedding more blood than most in the cause of saving Europe from itself and securing its freedoms - although some people forget this.

But Europe is no longer the world's most prosperous region. The priority task now is to build up links, many of which – in Britain's case - were so strong in the distant past, with what are becoming the world's most prosperous and dynamic areas of the world, but also with the smaller nations as well as the large ones, the struggling poor ones as well as the rapidly industrialising and increasingly high-tech ones. This is what an enlarged Commonwealth can deliver in a way that the European Union can never do, and never will do, and for which it lacks the reach and the right basic policy structure.

That is why Britain's external relations priorities deserve major re-alignment. And, as an afterthought, it is also why the UK Foreign and Commonwealth Office, the home of Britain's able and widely admired diplomatic service, ought now to be re-christened the Commonwealth and Foreign Office – the CFO not the FCO. Little changes can signify a lot.

CHAPTER ONE

Networks, The Microchip & The Conditions of the 21st Century

We are witnessing the biggest transformation in the international landscape since World War Two. Democracy, of a kind, has shifted visibly to the streets. A totally new global energy landscape is emerging. New international groupings are gaining significance alongside the old 20th century structures.

The information revolution, and the age of hyper-connectivity, mean that markets, wealth accumulations, influence and political power have all shifted. Network connectivity creates new degrees of immediacy and intimacy between states with which traditional diplomatic procedures cannot cope.

Networks have now replaced hierarchies and blocs. The advent of the information age, the new era of globalization and the huge consequential dispersal of information and power make old-style central authority and governance redundant. People power has now been e-enabled, humbling high authority while making the whole business of government much more difficult and subtle, and transforming not merely governments but relations between governments as well.

We live in a world seemingly falling apart yet paradoxically coming together as never before through the staggering power of constant and instant communications. Fragmentation versus super-connectivity – the two contradictory forces prevail simultaneously, bringing bewilderment and confusion to governments and governed alike.

English is the Hub Language of the 21st Century

Language allows people to weave networks by empowering them with the ability of communicate complex ideas, to coordinate their actions and establish commercial links. Language is the quintessential standard. It is the difference between the network of people who built the Tower of Babel and the fragmented network that was left after 'God' punished them with linguistic fragmentation. Today our world is still linguistically fragmented but that fragmentation is both declining and structured.

Ten thousand years ago humans spoke an estimated twelve thousand languages. An estimated six thousand are spoken world-wide today but most of the world's population communicates in a few global languages, and in many important on-line and off-line forums, including Twitter, Wikipedia and book translations, English has emerged as THE 'hub' language, bridging communication between languages. When Asian 'tiger' economies meet to plan progress they talk in English. Even Chinese corporations are instructing their workers to use English, as a more powerful medium for innovating ideas than their own Chinese. The English language has become the protocol of the cyber-entwined planet — a binding force par excellence with its own internal DNA.

Trade

Fundamental transformations have taken place in global trade, with many more on the way. These changes are influencing the sources and direction of trade and business linkages and their pattern and characteristics. And this in turn alters profoundly the competitive and comparative advantages of individual countries.

Thanks to the digital age and the stunning advances in almost total global connectivity modern trade is vastly more knowledge-laden and information-intensive than even a few years ago. The picture of export and import being solely a matter of giant container ships, manufacturers and raw materials now has to be revised. Services of every kind and digitalised information now form a larger part of international business than ever before. International trade links and supply chains have grown infinitely and rapidly more complex, outdating and invalidating the 20th century pattern of trade blocs and protected areas.

Furthermore, we are seeing globalisation of not just finished goods, but of processing, value-adding, and cross-border production networks. Conventional 20th century ambitions for protected single markets scarcely fit into these 21st century realities.

Almost all physical products now have a significant information and service content, whether via actual electronic parts, or via the machines which make them, the design input which shape them, the research behind them, the marketing and sales which transports and distributes them or endless other connections at every point in the production process.

This invalidates many of the assertions and figures to which we are constantly treated about sources, origins and destinations of international trade. In these new conditions of intense complexity and connectedness old-style multilateral trade negotiations, as well as regional bloc arrangements have stalled or become unravelled.

Rather than conventional tariff-based preferences and protected single markets the modern trading environment involves behind-the-border forms of integration and soft power relationships that have far more driving power in trade promotion.

Tariffs play a diminishing part in this changed world. Recently, for example, global trade in high tech products including advanced microchips, telecom products and GPS navigation has seen all import duties removed. Exchanges in these products alone, at some $1.3 trillion a year, surpass total world trade in textiles, iron and steel combined.

The remaining barriers to surmount lie far more in poor understanding, different cultural approaches and practices.

It used to be said that trade follows the flag. Today the situation is that trade, capital flows and investment - inward and outward - follow the softening up of markets through intertwining of cultures, language, social contacts, professions and common interests, all nowadays instantly and continuously connected. This can be more important in winning orders than any one-off trade mission.

This means that the new pattern and shape of trade is driven by powerful digital factors, by the greatly increased overlap between, what the sleepy statisticians still distinguish as, merchandise goods and export of services and information, by the phenomenal growth of the developing countries; by entirely new and different global value chains, by numerous new regional trade arrangements; and by climate concerns and upheavals in world energy and commitments to sustainable development.

Might No More

That which applies to money and which applies to communications also now applies to power. The amazing revolution in all things brought about by the information age, the internet, the explosion of consequent networking technologies and the combined chemistry of all this with global free markets, has not only dispersed knowledge, it has dispersed and re-allocated power and influence on a scale never before known. It is not just a question of capitalism recruiting billions of new adherents in booming Asia. The power to command and control, the power to create, and the power to destroy, have all being lifted out of hands of the old players. The cards had been re-dealt but the biggest players at the table seem only recently to have been noticing.

Nowhere on the surface were results of this apparent myopia more vivid and starker than what happened during the Iraq war. In speech after speech. President Bush and his colleagues explained how America would lead, how American strategy would reshape the region and how American military might – by many times the greatest defence arsenal in the world – must and would prevail. America's allies, notably Britain, would help. But with or without friends, America would overcome, America would 'surge' – that misleading verb – and America would succeed.

It is not just the White House and the Administration who saw things this way. The abused neo-conservatives by no means had a monopoly of misunderstanding in this area. Even the President's harshest critics assumed in their comments that America must lead the way out of the multiple crises which tortured the Middle East (See for example the Iraq Study Group, which, while critical of the Bush strategy, was steeped in the same assumptions about America's central role). And for those who had doubts, there was the hostile world outside to prove their point, a gigantic echo-box of anti-American sentiment. Did not all the noise from outside confirm what Americans already knew to be so - that they were the hegemon, the hyperpower, and that, like it or not, the world expected them to take centre stage and stay there?

The answers are now winging their way back and they are uncomfortable ones – so uncomfortable that it seems as though people just do not want to know. What was obvious to some from the outset of the present era was that democracy could not be delivered by overwhelming force, that 'democracy' was too variegated and subtle a concept to be packaged up and sent overseas and that overwhelming force could no longer overwhelm.

What remains much less obvious up to this very moment is why, beneath the surface, the entire structure of assumptions about America's power to control and influence world events has become flawed – in ways which were always bound to lead to the Iraqi fiasco and to strategic failure in the Middle East. This is what has yet to be grasped by a staggering number of people within American and British politics. For many it remains unthinkable. Yet it is beginning to seep into the debate – the cold reality which turns the American superpower and leadership dreams into a harsher American reality.

This is also the current Trump dilemma, although it is seldom depicted this way. Campaigning on the platform of American disengagement from 'foreign ventures' Donald Trump in office has found necessity and national prestige pulling the other way. Not only has he found it expedient and politically advantageous to authorise one-off interventions, such as the cruise missile strike in punishment against President Assad and his chemical weapons use. He has also been confronted with the ugly fact that over-rapid disengagement anywhere leaves both a dangerous vacuum and the stain of American humiliation as 'enemies' the US has been fighting and dying against, simply move back and take over, as in Afghanistan.

And what is this reality? It is that America is no longer in charge, command or control. It was not in charge in Iraq, it was not in charge in the Lebanon, it is not even in charge in the Israel-Palestine conflict, where so many commentators continue to call for it to 'take a lead' or 'do something'.

Incredible? Surely America is the biggest and the best, the boss nation, just as it has been since World War Two. No, sorry. The world is no longer organised that way. There are no boss nations. Washington is not Rome because there is no Rome. And America is not at the centre of the world because there is no centre, or not in the old power political sense. For reasons which are about to be explained and elaborated below the whole structure of relationships between nations and forces has moved on – from a vertical pattern of command and control – the big powers calling the shots – to a network pattern of connections and cooperation of infinitely greater subtlety and complexity.

In this new pattern, power has been miniaturised. The microchip has put lethal force, as well as power for creative good, into a thousand hands where one government or institution stood before. Ever more miniscule and yet more dangerous weapons have empowered groups far below the radar screen of nation states, rogue or otherwise, and levelled the playing field of projected power in ways utterly baffling to traditional thinking.

On the one side - gigantic standing armies and arsenals of missiles and nuclear warheads: on the other side, e-enabled, e-coordinated terror teams, tiny groups with high-tech weapons by their side, suicide squads, plotters stretching out to get their hands on nuclear material, even single individual fanatics – all empowered and with the muscle to take on giants, and to do so on terrifyingly equal terms.

Put bluntly, the world system of communication and cooperation has been changed totally and beyond recognition. Connectivity has transformed traditional notions of diplomacy, patterns of behaviour between nations and forms of international cooperation.

Twentieth Century Mindsets

Twenty years ago, we still saw the USA as the one dominant and, so we thought, invulnerable superpower. Our hopes for world peace rested, perhaps too heavily, on the United Nations. Yesterday we thought a united Europe could play a kind of bloc role in counter-balancing US might and protecting and projecting its member states' interests and influence.

Now we see that these perceptions were either wrong or too small. The new security challenges are totally global. Issues like terror, energy security, migration, disease control, climatic upheavals and disasters – all demand a world-wide network of approaches.

These have proven to be deeply difficult and complex changes to comprehend. They overturn the mindsets of fifty years past, indeed of the whole twentieth century. But until they are understood at the top, it will be not only American influence, reputation and foreign policy effectiveness which will remain hamstrung. It will be Britain's position as well. This is where the crucial changes have been missed, not just about the way foreign policy should be conducted by great powers but about the very latest phase in global affairs, which is quite unlike anything that has gone before. Does the possession of a still enormous stock of nuclear weapons nonetheless give America the residual power to dictate global strategy and guarantee national security? The reality is that nuclear warheads remain weapons of great danger but no longer weapons of power.

The prospect of their potential further proliferation is indeed one of the age's most serious issues. But nuclear warheads are weapons of deterrence between states, and to the extent that power has now drained away from states into other hands they are guarding the wrong gates. Furthermore, there is no such thing as an independent nuclear capability. The entire system of nuclear weapons ownership is interdependent. The only conceivable way of fighting nuclear terrorism is by establishing new alliances of the most intimate collaborative kind between both the existing nuclear powers, including obviously Russia and China, and the other 'declared' nuclear states, India and Pakistan, a category into which Israel, too, has to be pressed.

The former five 'existing nuclear powers' are now enmeshed in a network in which every move down or up, that is whether to decommission or to upgrade, has to be taken in total co-operation with others. Neither the Washington debate on America's role, nor the poorly-orchestrated debate in the UK on the upgrading of its Trident ballistic missile system seem to have taken any account of this new power distribution. Whether North Korea can be persuaded to shed its nuclear capabilities, or whether it can be assimilated into a new non-proliferation regime, remains to be seen. Either way it becomes an inseparable element in the global nuclear weapons network.

Asia the new Epicentre

If the American delusion is that size and military weight still mean global supremacy automatically, a similar kind of delusion distorts Europe's progress. The high vision is of the EU as an emergent bloc or superpower, both partner to and counterweight against the American behemoth, and all part of the grand Atlantic world, the Western world, the 'advanced' world.

In a staggeringly short space of time this has been invalidated and turned to dust. The centre of economic gravity is shifting fast - away from the old West and into Asia, with the three super-giants, a resurgent Japan, China and India at the heart of the new order. 'Asia is the epicentre of global politics and economics' declares Professor Chung Min Lee, one of the most respected authorities on East Asian security, as he opens his Trilateral Commission essay on the region, stating in a matter-of-fact way what he assumes all but the blindest now accept. The empires of the Atlantic world are no more. That phase of history is over.

Armies of statistics now support the Professor's assumption. In 2006 the JACIKS (Japan, ASEAN, China, India and Korea) accounted for 30 percent of the world's GNP, up from 24 percent three years earlier, and about the same now as the EU. The region produces around 30 percent of the world's total exports. China now imports more than the United States, as its huge growth rate sucks up oil and raw materials on a swelling scale, as well as products for its fast expanding and already enormous consumer markets.

The pattern of international capital flows is beginning to change. Investment which used to flow from West to East, from Europe to Asia, is going into reverse, with Chinese and Indian acquisitions in Europe, for example, mounting. At the same time a 'south-south' stream of investment is building up, with India, South Africa, Malaysia and Singapore all becoming substantial suppliers of capital to other (mainly Commonwealth) developing countries.

But this is not even half the story. The surging spread of free market capitalism has now brought, in the phrase of Clyde Prestowitz, the founder and President of the Economic Strategy Institute, 'three billion new capitalists' into the world system as power and opportunity have shifted eastwards. Of course, free markets were bound to spread anyway once the Communist bloc melted, and the old free world solidarity against Communism, which tended to bury commercial differences and restrictions, dissolved with it. But it is the seamless opportunities of the website world which turn American-led capitalism into what Edward Luttwak, an esteemed political scientist and strategist, christens turbo-capitalism and simply washes away America's high ground, making it a level player in the flattened scene.

The process goes much further. The wildfire spread of capitalism throughout Asia, mixing with Confucian and other ethics of saving, have produced a gigantic financing system which now directly supports the deficit-ridden West, and the United States in particular. Vast Asian dollar reserves, and a readiness to keep holding them and indeed carry on accumulating them, now underpins US economic growth. China's trillion dollar reserves, plus Japan's ($800 billion), plus Taiwan's and Hong Kong's hundreds of billions, and others besides, keeps the world's financial system in balance and in credit. Asia now literally holds the purse strings.

Easternisation

Like it or not, power is shifting. It is shifting to Asia, where China and India are about to become the strategic drivers of world affairs, and it is shifting even more to individuals at their keyboards and to the colossal opportunities for collaboration and initiative which have fallen into their hands. Of course, extrapolations and trajectory forecasts can often be wrong footed, it is true. When in the nineteen-nineties I described the coming rise of Asian power, not just in economic terms but in terms of superior moral and social cohesion, in a pamphlet entitled 'Easternisation', the subsequent hiccup caused by the Asian currency turmoil crisis was seized on by jeering critics (notably in the Times) to prove that this was all wrong.

It was wrong for about six months, before the far more powerful underlying trends, driven by the new ultra-accessible internet platforms, sent the fortunes and intentions of billions of motivated Asians soaring skywards again.

The same sort of chorus came on stage again with the collapse of the dotcom boom in 2000. Actually this event had the opposite effect, enabling multitudes of smaller enterprises to scoop up cheap communications infrastructures, such as fibre-optical networks, opening new free platforms (so-called open sourcing) and unleashing a torrent of new collaborative applications and procedures across the entire planet.

The effects went even further. Thanks to instantaneous interactivity on the web, and the google-isation of just about every activity and idea known to humankind, an entirely new pattern of supply chains has developed across the world. This is not just a matter of outsourcing chunks of production and processes from Western bases to India and elsewhere. Nor is it just simply a matter of western business investors off-shoring their plants and assets into the new growth areas with lower labour costs.

What have now mushroomed in the last few years are supply chains of infinite complexity and with items and ideas flowing in both directions – to and from the new economies and feeding the swelling Chinese and Asian markets just as much as the Western and Atlantic ones. Hundreds of millions of new middle-income Asian capitalists are now beginning to consume (as well as save) on a massive scale. Thus a single final product, whether a mere washing machine or an iPod or something as complex as an airliner, can be drawing in components and knowledge inputs from umpteen Western and Asian sources. National barriers and tariff walls are shrinking into insignificance and rearguard protective actions are now being fought through thinly disguised health and safety regulations (an EU speciality), desperately trying to catch up with the shuttle and swirl of transactions to and fro across the planet in every direction.

Self-organisation and collaboration at every level of humanity decimate the power of governments and former unchallenged authorities, the governments of the Atlantic powers very much included, and the USA very much included. Into individual hands the world-wide browser has tipped the power and capacity to create personalised worlds and intimate communities virtually independent of traditional social and official structures.

This is the context, super-global and super-local, in which elected nation state leaders have now to carve out a continuing role. Down the ladder go notions of national or regional strategic supremacy -no-one being supreme in a network world. Down the ladder go impulses towards exclusive (ourselves alone) national security – all parts of the global network being vulnerable and an attack on any city or society being an attack on all.

Down the ladder also go notions of national energy 'independence' – an idea of breathtaking unrealism being much toyed with by Trump's team, demonstrating yet again a deep ignorance of the now totally integrated nature of global energy supplies. And down the ladder go conceits about national and unilateral economic management and protection – all national economies not being interwoven and totally independent. By contrast, up the ladder come demands on national governments to be completely open and transparent, to deliver basic domestic services with infinitely greater efficiency and sensitivity, to respect local diversity and initiative far more readily, to ensure personal safety and security, and discourage lawlessness and crime, much more comprehensively. On the geo-political front up comes the priority mission to join ranks in coalitions and networks which minimize threats to national security and maximize the contribution which any nation can make to global peace and stability, thereby maximizing also any nation's sense of purpose, self-esteem and inner cohesion.

Friedman's World

Few better explanations exist of why and how this enormous transformation in the geo-political realities has taken place than that offered by the wonderfully perceptive writer, Thomas Friedman, in his book 'The World is Flat' . Friedman has arrived, in a way that his countrymen high in the Administration have not. Friedman now understands that for a whole range of reasons the globalisation process, and the communications revolution driving it, which the micro-chip set in motion some twenty-five years ago, has entered a third phase which changes everything.

This third phase is the one in which not only countries find themselves thrown into intimacy and interdependence on a wholly new scale, as walls and barriers tumble, and not only in which companies and businesses everywhere finds themselves drawn into entirely new global networks of services and supply chains. Thanks to the development of more and more Internet-based applications and possibilities the building of coalitions, projects and movements, good and bad, now falls into individual hands. Power becomes dispersed and flattened to an infinite degree, leaving central policy-planners, authorities and governments bereft of old instruments of authority and confronted by the need to adapt to completely new ones.

Of course none of this is entirely new. Over a decade ago seers like Manuel Castells were describing in immense detail how the informational (he called it) revolution would transform not only government but the whole structure of global relationships. And to that some of us added our own warnings that as power was dispersed, and as capitalism became totally globalised (as predicted quite accurately long ago by Karl Marx), Western government ascendancy would pass to markets, to rising societies away from the Atlantic basin, as well as to malign and dangerous groupings in a near anarchic pattern .

But the point is that Friedman has not only got there but is able to put the case to his peers with unparalleled punch and persuasion, which probably explains why he wins Pulitzer prizes, left right and centre, and this is surely a cause of cautious rejoicing – two cheers with maybe a third to come.

Yesterday's Europe

The direct external implications for both Europe and for the United Kingdom of these fundamental re-alignments of power, of influence and of trends in human affairs could not be clearer. No integrated regional bloc will hold together under the impact of the world-wide system of supply chain production and disintegrated power which the internet and the web have ushered into being.

If Germany, or any other European nation, wants security and protection of its civil society against terrorist attacks, if it wants energy security and real and lasting benefits for its citizens, as well as a fully restored reputation as a responsible global player, it should be looking not only at greater European regional co-operation on local issues, which is always desirable, and not only at good relations with the United States, which are always worth having. More important now than either of those goals is the need to burnish relations with the rising powers and markets of Asia, where the key decisions will be made which will make or break world-wide terrorism, stabilize the Middle East and lift tens of millions out of poverty fastest.

If Germany, or any other European nation, is concerned about climate security, as we all are, it should be looking to China and India for direct cooperation in fighting global warming, where decisions far more influential in cleaning the atmosphere than any carbon emissions trading scheme in Europe will have to be made. If Germany, or any other European nation, wants bigger markets it should be looking at the already huge consumer power of South-East Asia, at Chinese markets and at internet markets. The mantra that the EU itself is the world's biggest market gets repeatedly asserted. It is no longer true.

If Germany wants more secure energy supplies it should look north to Norway, reduce its overdependence on Russia and resume nuclear power station building, with the latest and safest technologies, rather than put its faith in an EU common energy policy which will never happen.

The search should be on in every European nation for the new networks and linkages which will bring its citizens the most benefits in the new conditions. Time and energies spent trying to achieve unachievable ambitions for a united EU foreign policy and for a European state's place in the sun (shades of Kaiser Wilhelm the Second), or stretching for dreams of the EU as a new superpower are far better spent reaching out and associating with the nodes of powering in the new global network.

Amongst member states France has shown the most awareness of the new priorities – in Asia and elsewhere - whilst continuing with admirable dexterity to 'play' the EU scene and use the EU in ways best designed to assist France's aspirations (not least, to prevent the resurgence of an over-mighty Germany).

In India, Australia, New Zealand, in Japan, in the oil and gas–rich Gulf States, in Norway and the Baltic, in Poland and other parts of central Europe, our friends are waiting for us and people are asking 'where are the British?'. These are not only the countries that want to work with us and think broadly like us about the world. They are the network of the future and the powerhouses of the future. Together with giant China they are the areas where economic dynamism flourishes and to which the centre of global economic gravity is shifting. That's where the action is going to be and that is where the British, with their long history of adventure and their vast global reach, should also be.

Conclusion

A new constellation of nations, powers, influences and forces has emerged. Even what it means to be a democratic state has changed in the instant communication age and e-enabled street protest. Generally, a vast global bouleversement is taking place. The developing states are fast becoming the developed.

The poor are becoming the less indebted while the rich, the so-called 'advanced' nations, are mired deeper in debt than ever before in history. The savings of the East and the South are coming to the rescue of the North and the West.

This is an era in which information and communications technology has transformed almost every aspect of human existence, empowering groups, organizations, interests, markets and indeed personal lives as never before in history. In effect it has redistributed both influence and power – and in both good ways and bad.

The good side of the story is that hundreds of millions of people across the world have been given new hope and new opportunities. Governments everywhere have had to listen more closely to the people, women have found a stronger voice and place, and the participation of the rising nations of Asia, Africa and Latin America in global improvement and expanding trade, investment and prosperity has been vastly expanded.

The bad side is that power has also slipped into the hands of non-state groups with evil intent, determined to overthrow all authority and challenge all legitimacy, as now tragically evidenced in many parts of the Arab world.

We are in the midst of an all-embracing technology-drive revolution that is transforming business activity and transforming world trade in the developed and the developing world alike. Analytics, automation, the Internet of Things, use of amazing new lightweight materials — all these developments are rippling through economic life. Within this revolutionary new context it so happens, without any master plan or ideological impulse, that the Commonwealth network emerges as the ideal platform – the self-associating and non-hierarchical type structure which is utterly suited to the digital age. And this becomes so not just in terms of business and trade but in terms of common culture, common legal procedures, common attitudes, underpinned by common working language, common security interest, common values and aspirations and a hundred other linkages of likemindedness and soft power intimacy.

Some call it the fourth industrial revolution. Some call it the second globalisation wave. But I call it the hour of the Commonwealth network, linking up no less than 2.4 billion peoples, a third of the world population, larger than any nation – even larger than Facebook!

CHAPTER TWO

. The UK's Foreign Policy & The Need for Change

This is at once a story, a plea and a proposal.

The story is how British foreign policy lost its way in the early years of the twenty first century, seriously weakening Britain's reputation and influence, as well as the nation's internal sense of unity, security and purpose.

The plea is for our policy leaders to make a renewed effort to understand the deep forces which have changed the nature and pattern of international relations and changed the way in which national security is safeguarded and influence projected – an understanding which has eluded not just minds in London but much of the Washington establishment as well, with visibly disastrous results.

The proposal is that without in any way betraying our friends, without ceasing to be America's good partner, without ceasing to be good Europeans, we find a restored place for Britain in this transformed global pattern, using our historical experience, instincts and ties, our position and our national talents once again to the full.

The EU and British Foreign Policy

Taunted by MEPs in 2005 the Prime Minister, Tony Blair, angrily asserted, that 'our future lies in Europe'. 'They are our colleagues and partners', he added.

Of course he was right that geographically Europe is our region and neighbourhood, and was right, too, if he meant that the health, stability and prosperity of this wonderful continent is very much in Britain's interest. We must always be – and actually have nearly always been – good Europeans and we must make big sacrifices (as we have certainly done in the past) to this end.

But, alas, the former Prime Minister meant much more than that, and this is where the flaws and fissures in his stance, and in the whole shape of British foreign policy, began. What he believed, and many like him, is not only that our future lay in the European Union (not the same as, although easily confused with, Europe) but that our international stance, purposes and interests, should be looked after by the institutions of the European Union and subsumed in a broader common EU foreign policy.

'We must work' said the policy-makers, 'through our European partners'. That was our destiny.

In other words, he and others who thought like him (and they existed in all three major parties) saw British foreign policy as being primarily to contribute to the larger EU positioning and to making that larger policy work effectively. This remained the central, collective belief as well of the Foreign and Commonwealth Office. The strategic priority, as set out in FCO documentation, was to help make the EU foreign policy a reality, because that indeed was where our future was said to be.

'Working with our European partners' has been the mantra of FCO thinking for three decades. The essence of British foreign policy has been that while bilateral links between Britain and other countries remain important, and our links with America especially important (and once given new life by the Blair-Bush bond), the main and central concern had been 'getting Europe right'. It is to the Europe of ever closer union and deepening integration that Britain's 'destiny' was supposed to beckon us and it was through the EU collectively that our relations with the world, including trans-Atlantic relations, were best worked out, or so they said.

Although there was a big wobble over the Iraq invasion, and another one over the Constitution fiasco, that central idea remained for many years alive and well in London, largely embodied in the concept of a Common Foreign and Security Policy (CFSP), with Javier Solana and later Federica Mogherini, the EU's would-be Foreign Minister , as its herald and instrument.

However, throughout that period the brutal truth that no one wanted to hear was that the EU common foreign policy, in so far as it existed at all, was not serving or protecting

British interests in modern conditions very well. With twenty-eight marvellously diverse nations, and twenty-eight different perspectives on the world, anything pushed through the CFSP filter was bound to be muffled, fuzzy and a fertile source of misunderstanding. This is so whether the issue was Iraq or Iran or Israel-Palestine or Lebanon, or Russia and how to handle Mr Putin, or China and weapons, or Turkey and enlargement, or the UN, or above all, how to talk to the Americans.

Few would disagree that nowadays effective foreign policy needs partners and allies – more so than ever in this network age. Even the hardest line go-it-alone merchants in Washington now acknowledge that.

However, the EU did not provide the UK with the right partners. As the centre of economic gravity in the world moves to Asia, was the EU helping us in our relations with China? With India? With the developing world in an equal and friendly relationship? With the turbulent Middle East? With Russia? With the unstable Central Asian republics? And above all, with mighty America, our traditional ally, seemingly so powerful and yet also so vulnerable?

The briefest reality check should tell us that not only was EU policy of little positive benefit in any of these areas, it had become a serious hindrance. The trans-Atlantic relationship was particularly worrying. In EU hands it had fallen to the lowest point for decades. Far from the EU calming and clarifying trans-Atlantic disputes by speaking with one clear voice, it seemed to be amplifying them so that what were once containable second-class differences were being elevated into damaging first class rows. This was not at all in Britain's interest.

The Bridge of Dreams

Sixty years ago, Britain fulfilled the steadying partner and friend role to America – at least up to a point, although as Winston Churchill found out, this became very difficult as America began calling all the shots in conducting Allied policy in World War Two. Then there was Kennedy's twin pillars idea in the Cold War context, although it was never a phrase that could stand too much analysis. NATO, too, was going to be the binding link of equals.

However, as the conditions of the world changed, so did the relationship. Under Blair, Britain was supposed to become a bridge between an America confident in its continuing task of leadership in the age of globalisation and a Europe increasingly united, purposeful and dynamic.

This would put the British in – yes – a pivotal role, at the epicentre of world events, wonderfully positioned between Pax Americana and Pax Europa. Gone would be the resigned or outright defeatist talk of Britain as the Athens to Washington's Rome, so widespread in the days of Harold Macmillan. And gone would be fears of Britain as the isolated offshore island of Europe, the other great terror of the Macmillan era, and one which still stalks the corridors of the Foreign Office in London to this day.

To work in practice this vision would require a) that such a bridge was needed and would be used, b) that America remained firm and resolute in its global purposes, c) that Europe had a clear way forward as a cohesive and effective force on the world stage, and d) that the Atlantic alliance, linking the two continental entities (and their destinies) of the United States and the European Union, was still the dominant, agenda-setting partnership in global affairs.

Unfortunately, none of these conditions now apply. The bridge idea was perhaps fanciful from the start, a left-over vanity from history and the Second World War.

Sir Christopher Meyer's readable but much criticised account of British Prime Ministerial and other visits to Washington brings home the vainglorious absurdity of these dreams, describing vividly, as it does, the mixture of obsequiousness and awe-struck deference shown by the British visitors in Washington to the President and his entourage. As Sir Christopher implies, it only needed the over-eager Mr Blair to promise undying, loyalty and unconditional commitment, to be 'with you at the first and we'll be with you to the last' for Washington policy-makers to conclude that capture was complete and little further attention to any 'conditions' or qualifications from the British was warranted, except, of course, the ritual diplomatic politesse. The Washington thought bubble has been easy to read all along. Nice to have the British on board, it goes, but no need to take much notice of what they say.

New Relationships & New Partners

Fast forward to today and for all its armed might America desperately needs real and trusted friends, not just to fulfil its awesome world responsibilities but to deliver security to its own citizens. Even the go-it-alone warriors in Washington are now coming to recognise this. Even President Trump has felt compelled to explain that his 'America First' ambition does not mean America alone.

Less easy to swallow in Washington is the fact that true friendship and support mean more than tick-the-box compliance. True friendship means frankness, candour, criticism when appropriate (as long as it is basically constructive and not just born of ill will), compete mutual trust and respect and, even if occasionally, a restraining hand.

The EU does not get to Square One in any of these roles. The rhetoric of EU-US partnership may continue, but even if poor Javier Solana or Federica Mogherini could have articulated a common European policy towards the Americans, which they could not, why should they get more than a cold nod from the Administration? Why should Washington give a respectful hearing to an entity which it sees – not without justification – as basically anti-American, sounding less and less like a friend and partner and increasingly like a constantly hostile bloc – a transatlantic neighbour from hell, picking a quarrel on every issue, large or small.

Just as the United States has gradually discovered that it cannot go-it-alone on the new international scene, so the same applies even more strongly to the United Kingdom.

Partners and allies are required in an interdependent world, and partners with sufficient clout and cohesion for Washington to want to listen to them and to have to listen to them. Neither condition applies in the case of the EU, whose basically anti-American stance makes them unwelcome visitors in Washington and worthless interlocutors, having divided views on almost everything, stagnant economies and a minimal force contribution to make to world policing.

A whole army of European leaders, experts, officials and apologists have wasted years, as well as forests of paper, chasing after a flawed belief that Europe can somehow be welded into a solid bloc that will carry weight on the world stage, counter-balance American hegemony and confront Asian challenges.

These people seem not to have grasped that networks have now replaced hierarchies and blocs. They seem not to have understood that the advent of the information age, the new era of globalization and the huge consequential dispersal of information and power make old-style central authority and governance redundant. People power has now been e-enabled, humbling high authority while making the whole business of government much more difficult and subtle, and transforming not merely governments but relations between governments as well.

This applies as much to the EU as to the nation states within it. Trying to recreate the EU in the image of the 200-year-old United States was a foolish mistake . It was worse, because it has distracted the Europeans from the real new tasks to which they should be applying their combined strength -- namely combating the rise of global terror, crime and the warped power of fanaticism, which also derives its dangerous growth from the information revolution. This is the dark side of globalization.

Quite simply, while effective foreign policy needs partners and allies– more so than ever in this network age – our main European neighbours were the wrong partners and the CFSP tied us into the wrong partnership.

But now the question to be answered is where we look for the partnership or grouping which the American giant really will listen to and work with, and from which the world, and especially Britain, would so obviously benefit.

The starting point is to identify the countries which really are America's best friends, who are not all screwed up with anti-American resentments, and which would be comfortable with a solid-two-way strategic relationship with the great superpower, not in a poodle capacity but at an equal and full-trust level.

A structure is to hand which could form at least the underpinning for such a platform. This structure, or network, is the 53 nation Commonwealth, which far from being a marginal institution, full of good works and nostalgia, is now emerging as the ideal model for international relations in the new conditions the world faces.

Today's Commonwealth now contains thirteen of the world's fastest growing economies, including the most potent emerging markets. Outside the USA and Japan, the

key cutting edge countries in information technology and
e-commerce are all Commonwealth members. The new
'jewel in the Commonwealth Crown' turns out to be the old
jewel, dramatically re-polished and re-set, namely booming
India, the world's largest democracy with a population set
to exceed China's. This presents a picture so far removed
from the old image of the Commonwealth, bogged down
in demands for more aid and arguments about South Africa
(or latterly Zimbabwe) that many sleepy policy makers find
it simply too difficult to absorb. The unloved ugly duckling
organisation has grown almost overnight into a true swan. Or
to use a different metaphor the Commonwealth of today and
tomorrow has been described as 'The Neglected Colossus'. It
should be neglected no longer.

In addition to Commonwealth countries, in Europe the
front-runners are Poland, the brilliant little Baltic three, the
Czechs and maybe the Italians, if they keep their own house
in order. Norway, too, small but probably now sitting on the
biggest oil and gas reserves outside the Middle East up north
in the Barent Sea, also belongs in the group who are pro-
NATO, pro-American, but not uncritically so, and uneasy
about EU global pretensions.

Admittedly this would be a geographically scattered
grouping, not the sort of regional alliance our history books
used to talk about. But in the age of the internet who cares?
As partners they are only one click away from each other.
Sit down this big and powerful grouping round the table
with America's leaders and one would immediately have a

partnership of real equality, frankness and mutual respect, with enough influence and clout as well to restrain America's wobblier impulses.

This would be a league or network of willing nations, races and cultures, able to establish an effective framework for world stability in ways which the soured and discredited EU-US 'partnership' is no longer capable of doing. Britain's new foreign policy priority should be to build up this new kind of alliance, instead of muttering about pivots, bridges with Europe and the like. The British remain good Europeans, as they have been all along, having saved Europe from itself more than once. But when it comes to twenty first century strategic linkages and alliances, the time has come to think entirely afresh.

A Turning of the Tides?

Unlike Blair, Cameron perceived that while America was a mighty economy, its size no longer delivered influence. New power centres and alliances had grown. His conservative government was guided by a bold and profound critique of American misunderstandings of the new world, and an equally bold critique of the wrong direction in which too many were trying to take the EU.

Cameron was aware that the UK must not be hobbled in its international connections and contributions either by Washington's two-dimensional visions nor by the limp attitudes of our European partners, as they struggled in vain to reach a common foreign policy.

For both Cameron and Osborne, wooing China was one of the biggest foreign policy goals. In 2015, our then Chancellor called for China to become our second largest trading partner. Earlier that year, the Prime Minister announced that "I want us to be nothing less than the modern world's most open, trade-minded nation. To do that, we must tap into markets outside Europe; to look to the Commonwealth and beyond."

Finally, Whitehall was beginning to grasp that the big economic prizes for Britain in the future lay elsewhere than simply Europe. Tellingly, Osborne was the first British Chancellor for many years to attend Commonwealth finance minister's meetings. They knew that it was in the vast new markets of Asia, Africa and even Latin America that our export underperformance had to be reversed and in which Britain would either survive or succumb.

Brexit, Britain & The Commonwealth

We are now beginning to focus back on the most important international family we have, for two reasons.

Firstly, with Brexit in prospect attention has turned, sometimes a bit shamefacedly, to the trade possibilities in Commonwealth markets - possibilities which were not only caste aside back in 1972 but studiously ignored by London policy-makers ever since.

Suddenly, all the talk is of making new links and refreshing old ties. Free Trade Agreements are to be eagerly sought on all sides. Commonwealth countries who received the cold shoulder back in 1972 can be forgiven for a certain scepticism. But the hope is that the snubbed ones – especially those that have developed vastly richer consumer markets in recent decades - will forgive, forget and cooperate. As with those BA Business Class seats, the dividing screen has been briskly lowered and its smiles for the family all round.

The second reason is a mixture of serendipity and prescience. Back in November 2015, at the Malta. Commonwealth Heads of Government meeting, Britain agreed – at the time with a good deal of pushing from some of us and without much enthusiasm – to host the next Commonwealth summit in the Spring of 2018. Scroll forward to late 2016 and in London it all looks different. The Commonwealth Summit becomes a major staging event in the great British re-positioning, away from the EU as Britain's destiny and towards Britain as a global power in a network world. The Commonwealth ceases to be just one more international body in the foreign policy portfolio and becomes a central part of the future strategic picture. A handful of Civil servants in the Foreign Office is briskly replaced by an army of officials in a new Cabinet Office unit charged with taking the whole affair forward and coordinating activity right across Whitehall and the private sector.

Some protesting voices and scepticism there is bound to be, especially from within the bureaucracy. One civil servant is reported to have likened the shift to 'Empire 2.0'. But overall these administrative changes are good and very encouraging. Yet I believe there are deeper reasons still to explain the new and growing sense of relevance of the Commonwealth network. These lie not in Brexit, or just in renewed British commitment and interest but in something much deeper and with far more global significance.

Living by our wits on a small-ish, although still beautiful island, and its appendages, in a subtly evolved union of kingdoms which has grown over centuries and which only the most shallow and short-sighted want to pull apart, we can least afford to stay tied to the tramlines of past thinking about the international order and the nature and distribution of global power, and least afford to pass up casually the huge advantages which by good fortune have come our way from past legacies.

A New Priority

Britain badly needs a new foreign policy appropriate to the twenty-first century. Our interests are not being protected and promoted as they should be. Nor is our contribution to global peace, stability and prosperity being maximised or being as effective as it could or should be.

As far as possible we want to manage our economy independently and flexibly. But everyone knows that we are interdependent as well, in fact more so than ever nowadays. It is therefore a crucial part of sound economic policy to make sure we have the right external partners and to handle all the external influences on our lives and work in the right way.

But today we have the wrong partners and we are under the wrong influences. We have let our interest and our foreign policy dangerously diverge. We put our faith in our so-called European partners to promote and protect our national interests. But in reality they were doing us no favours at all – while our interests increasingly lay elsewhere. We proudly claimed to be members of every conceivable international organisation and alliance, but this blinded us as to where our real interests lie.

It is time for Britain to review and alter her alliances radically and work much more closely with our true friends, which may not be the same thing as our geographical neighbours. Nor is it the same thing as obediently agreeing, poodle-like, with the Washington Administration. We are America's friends, but not its uncritical friends.

CHAPTER THREE

Our Real Friends

Where to Look? Where then should the UK in the twenty first century be looking for real friends and allies on whom it can rely and together with whom it can make a truly effective input to global strategy and stability? The neglected answer lies on its doorstep. The Commonwealth, a voluntary association of 53 independent states, operating on an advanced, 'open' system of cooperation and networking, both formal and informal, offers the basis for a structure of remarkable potential and relevance to the conditions of the twenty-first century. Here is a quite extraordinarily latticed association of like-minded states, trans-continental, multi-faith, embracing rich and poor and, which sits before Britain's eyes, almost virtually on a plate (or more precisely with its headquarters and secretariat in the heart of London at Marlborough House).

These connections stretch right across the regions and hemispheres and also right into the everyday life of millions of people in thousands of local communities. Yet where is the political philosophy, or the policy or programme derived from that philosophy, which even recognises their existence, let alone their growing role?

A nation with a developed 'global' outlook and policy, geared to today's conditions, ought to give immense attention and encouragement to this kind of network pattern of international relations. It is clearly the most effective way to project national concerns, defend national interests and address international issues in a globalised environment.

The new premium on network relations favours some organisations which seemed less useful in the past. A typical example is the Commonwealth whose members now form the perfect inter-governmental and voluntary network and under whose umbrella literally hundreds of non-governmental and semi-official Commonwealth bodies create a web of common purpose unequalled in any other global arrangements.

Far from being a run-down club, held together by nostalgia and decolonisation fixations, today's Commonwealth now contains thirteen of the world's fastest growing economies, including the most potent emerging markets. Outside the USA, Japan and China, the key cutting edge countries in information technology and e-commerce are all Commonwealth members.

By accident and luck, this is the kind of arrangement which is now almost perfectly tailored to fit into the new global scene and offers both its members and the wider international community an ideal platform on which to work together in face of new threats and opportunities both as power passes to Asia and is scattered across Thomas Friedman's flatter world.

Because the Commonwealth is founded on respect for nation states, each following its own path, yet recognising the imperative of interdependence, constant adjustment can take pace to new challenges, with partnerships and coalitions being swiftly tailored to each new scene. This answers three dilemmas.

The first is that people want more than ever in an age of remote globalisation, to develop their own identities, to have countries and localities to love and defend and take pride in. They recognise the fact of interdependence but they long equally for ownership and a degree of independence. Superior ideas of supra-national government and super-states, along with sweeping dismissals of the relevance of the nation state, can play no part in resolving these deep and competing needs, and indeed utterly fail to do so when imposed by well-intentioned integrationists, as in the case of the EU.

Second, rigid bloc alliances cannot keep up with the kaleidoscope of change. The more that the European Union tries to draw its members into a unified political and military bloc the less effective it becomes. The more that the world is seen as clinging to a structure of blocs established in rivalry to each other the more the real criss-cross network of bilateral linkages between nations is neglected. Yet it is just this new and more flexible pattern which provides far the best guarantee of stability and security.

Third, the new texture of international relations is made up not just of inter-governmental and official contacts but of a mosaic of non-governmental and sub-official agencies and organisations. This takes time to grow, but grow it has under the Commonwealth canopy into an amazing on organizations and alliances between the professions, the academic and scholastic worlds, the medical, educational, scientific and legal communities and a host of other interest groups linked together across the 53 nation Commonwealth Group.

Long Neglect

It might be thought that the obvious potential offered by the Commonwealth network model would be at the heart of thinking in London on Britain's need to re-position. One might have thought that although today's actual Commonwealth secretariat is weak and under-funded the opportunities for the Commonwealth to raise it game and be developed into an instrument of huge benefit and relevance for all its members, but especially for Britain in view of past associations and present skills, would be central to ruminations and scenario planning in the corridors of the Foreign and Commonwealth Office.

One might also have thought that Britain would see the Commonwealth network, strengthened and expanded, as an ideal circuit by which to connect far more closely with the ASEAN nations and their markets.

But one would be quite wrong. The realisation of the Commonwealth's potential in the newly emerged world conditions is only beginning to be comprehended. As for stronger interest in ASEAN, officials from Singapore and other dynamic Asian centres sigh and admit that they have failed to engage British interest in their region. For the last two decades the notice on the door has said, "Gone to Brussels. Busy with our European Partners. Call Back Later".

Our foreign policy thinking apparatus has remained locked in the world of blocs and alliances of the past, and up until 2016 was paralysed by the conviction that an integrated EU was 'the answer' and something in which Britain would get 'left behind' at its peril. The idea of building on the ready-made structure of the future which the Commonwealth offers still appears beyond reach for many.

Yet the policy-makers have been curiously slow in grasping this. The Commonwealth network potential has barely been recognised by British officials and international experts, while the old instinct, which is either to leave international tasks untackled or to delegate them upwards to unaccountable international bodies, has remained dismally resilient. There can be no question that the list of tasks and duties requiring a global approach is getting much bigger - from financial regulation to environmental control and from security, both internal and external, to health and safety standards. Nor can it be contested that these issues have to be handled by organisations larger than the nation state.

The long-standing neglect of the Commonwealth, or perhaps more precisely the traditional mixture of boredom and disinterest, – both in the higher reaches of British government and part of the Foreign Office, the British media and the British public – had three origins.

First, the Commonwealth in days gone by seemed preoccupied with bashing the UK, criticising its colonial and post-colonial role, demanding more aid and generally making the British the focus of blame for under-performance in numerous Commonwealth member countries, especially in Africa. To British opinion much of this criticism seemed unfair and unreasonable and ignored the record of relatively successful de-colonisation.

Second, the Commonwealth seemed to offer no obvious economic attractions, while the original European Community clearly did. The days of Empire preference were gone, emerging Commonwealth markets refused to emerge (with the exception of Singapore) and foreign investment looked elsewhere.

Third, the Commonwealth, whilst retaining the British Queen as its titular head, seemed to have no organisational hierarchy or drive at the centre. It appeared incapable of turning talk into real influence and action.

As we shall see, the first of these perceptions fell out of date in the nineteen–nineties or earlier. The second has more recently been overtaken by major shifts in the shape and direction of the global economy. The third view may be correct analytically, but is now metamorphosing into a strength, and not a weakness at all, in the network age. In a space of time seemingly much too short for the attitudes of the policy-making establishment to catch up the Commonwealth has changed almost beyond recognition. We are now looking not at a nostalgia-tinted grouping of slow-growing or stagnant economies but at one of the most successful and relevant collections of nations ever, with some of the central drivers of economic growth in its midst.

For what today's Commonwealth is developing into is something quite different from the past. It is becoming the necessary network of the twenty-first century – a set of relationships between nations large and small, and between their peoples, which is not provided by any other multilateral institution, but which is increasingly needed and, as the membership waiting room confirms, sought after. As virtual linkages spread, almost to the point of creating virtual nations, and as hard physical relationships become more complicated, the outstanding characteristic of the Commonwealth is that it spans both worlds – the actual and the virtual, the public and the private, the official or governmental, and the non-governmental linked and e-enabled world of markets, professions and peoples. As with quantum particles, it is possible within the Commonwealth to be in two places and two states at the same time.

The hub and spoke model of the past typically put Britain at the centre of a sort of wheel with lines going out to all our Commonwealth partners, now 53 in number (with more lining up to join). The network and cluster concept is quite different. Instead of links from a central point to the various points on the rim there emerges a fantastic network of linkages without any particular centre.

Is this possible or practical? Yes, in the digital age it now is. Of course some of the linkages will be stronger between bigger trading partners and associates and some will be thinner, but the modern network is a pattern without a dominant or dictating centre. Furthermore because networks talk to other networks all the time it is a continuously growing system, so that unless one is deliberately exclusive fantastic series of linkages opens up ready and in effect lead to networking the entire planet.

And furthermore again, while borders will of course remain, time-consuming impediments to trade flows will be largely eradicated by split-second digital clearance. Decisions from official authorities will become instant. Customs officers and much of the paraphernalia of frontiers will become redundant.

All networks of course require a framework or what used to be called in the language of the past a hierarchy of control and governance. Today the old links about which we are talking provide the framework, (in some cases, such as Hong Kong, quite regardless of national boundaries). Meanwhile, the new ties provide the explosion of connections and gravitational effects which now govern international trade, made vastly more powerful day by day by the emergence of new technologies such as block chains which allow the ever-multiplying part of the microchip to handle and validate the commands, wishes and opinions of tens of millions of people instantaneously. There has been nothing like it ever before in human history. Even the largest super-powers have to accept nowadays that they are part of this ever-evolving global network of networks.

Very few planned or foresaw this. On the contrary, a widespread view in the later decades of the twentieth century was that the Commonwealth had lost its relevance. It was a club of the past, a family of yesterday, held together by little more than nostalgia. Yet contrary to expectations, what is emerging instead from the old pattern is something that fits amazingly closely with the future and with the technological revolution in which the world is now caught up.

First, the Commonwealth today, far from being a backward-looking coterie of states, is proving (to the surprise of some) to be a living network of relationships and like-minded values and principles that stretches across all continents – Asia, Africa, Europe, the Americas – and across almost all religions, at a time when global reach is essential to tackle global problems. The great themes of democracy, human rights, good governance and the rule of law, the aspirations of all humankind, have found in the modern Commonwealth a fresh and resilient means of propagation in the network age.

Second, the Commonwealth, again to the surprise of some, is one of the fastest-developing associations of nations in the world – in some parts faster even than China – and contains at least seven of the most dynamic, knowledge-driven economies in the world. As the west's trade and investment tilts away from Europe and the Atlantic, and towards rising Asia and

Africa, the Commonwealth network becomes more and more relevant for all its citizens in hard commercial terms, meaning jobs and investment in an age short of both.

Third, the Commonwealth survives and attracts new members when the world's other multilateral organisations, designed for the twentieth century, are failing us and in deep trouble. It provides scope for a real North–South dialogue on equal rather than patronising terms.

Fourth, in an age of small states, many of them feeling bypassed by global trends and tossed in the storms of world economic volatility, the Commonwealth platform offers a life-raft of opportunity and influence, where smaller voices get a bigger hearing, and the problems of smaller states receive genuine attention and consideration, notably in meeting the severe challenges of climate change, energy scarcity, food and water needs, and other escape routes from poverty. It gives Britain yet another chance to recover its once strong reputation for helping the smaller and weaker states of the planet, to be a source of supportive partnership and not pressure, free of any suggestion of dominance, exploitation or control.

At least potentially, the Commonwealth is thus emerging as the kind of forum in which richer and faster-growing countries and the poorer and smaller nations can speak on equal terms, in which people from different faiths can sit down and discuss their problems calmly (there are 500 million Muslims in the Commonwealth), and in which almost all members are seriously committed – or under steady pressure to be committed to good governance and to contributing to global peace and stability, rather than pursuing vendettas against America and 'the West'.

Fifth, the Commonwealth, unlike most other multinational organisations and combinations of states in today's world, is an assembly of peoples, not just of governments. Its most visible aspect may be heads of government gathering together, but beneath the official layer lies a vast substructure of alliances and groups, interests and professional bodies, civil societies and voluntary associations, all proudly carrying the Commonwealth badge.

If there is a single explanation for what has occurred to galvanize the modern Commonwealth it probably lies in the microchip, meaning the information revolution and the globalization process to which it is linked. Quite simply the Commonwealth network of countries, societies, interests and peoples has been brought to a new life by the phenomenon of instant global communication and connection.

This has occurred, and is occurring at all levels, from the individual to the governmental, and from the humblest group or organisation to the largest state. The latticework of live associations and linkages described above stretching across the whole 53 nation Commonwealth network on a staggering scale, has become wired up as never before, enabling almost continuous dialogue and creative exchange – a kind of unending concerto of co-operation and common identification and purpose.

It is true that much of this extraordinary network was there before. But in the new age of transparency and accountability world-wide, in which the web and the mobile phone-camera open almost every window of activity and social trend, this meshwork of contacts has been given a kind of blood transfusion. In effect the Commonwealth 'badge' has become a sought-after asset – an entreé to the community of trust, reliability and transparency which the world's investors and traders constantly search for. This is certainly one explanation of the fact that countries with only a remote link with the old British sphere, or none at all, have either already joined the Commonwealth, or aspire to do so, or at least seek to link up with its various supporting groups.

Of course, the global communications miracle is not the only transforming force in the Commonwealth network. It interacts closely with the other key binding factor – a common language, and embedded within it the DNA of common attitudes, assumptions, instincts, manners, ideas of what constitutes humour and ways of looking at the world which a language contains and purveys. Because the language is English the origins of many of these things go back to British traditions and values, but by no means all. The Britishness factor has long since become enriched by and interwoven with many other cultures, Asian, African and Caribbean, in some cases much older and more powerful than the traces of the British legacy.

The Family

Marlborough House in the Mall is the visible centre of the Commonwealth. It makes a good setting, with its superb murals commissioned by Sarah Churchill, first duchess of Marlborough, and its echoes of a glittering past as the home of 'Bertie', Prince of Wales (later Edward VII). From here 'the Marlborough House set' radiated out and enlivened Victorian London society (some would say a little too much). Here, down the years, Secretary Generals such as Arnold Smith, Sonny Ramphal, Chief Enayaku, Don McKinnon, Kamelesh Sharma and currently Baroness Scotland of Ashtal have been able to look out across the world on the Commonwealth family.

But appearances are deceptive. What you see is not what you any longer get. The Secretariat is not a head office because the modern Commonwealth is not managed, or led, from the top down. The strength comes from below, from the dizzying range of Commonwealth-oriented organisations and initiatives across the world which the internet has now connected and enlivened. The Commonwealth Parliamentary Association brings parliamentarians and legislators together from every corner of the Commonwealth. Alongside this global parliamentary convocation are the Commonwealth-wide organisations promoting parliamentary administration and techniques of accountability, as well as sharing lessons learnt, at Westminster and elsewhere, about the operation of committees of Parliament, not least the Public Accounts Committee.

Around this parliamentary network, other main 'pillar' organisations proliferate, such as the Commonwealth Foundation, the umbrella body for civil societies, the Commonwealth Enterprise and Investment Forum, thriving and expanding as never before as intra-Commonwealth trade and investment grows. Or there are the legal bodies underpinning the vital common law pattern of the Commonwealth, such as the Commonwealth Lawyers Association, or the Commonwealth Magistrates and Judges Association, all in turn spreading common standards of judicial administration.

The other professions – the doctors, accountants, surveyors, planners, nurses, educationalists, journalists, broadcasters, social workers – all have their Commonwealth networks. There is also Commonwealth Connects, a strategic digital initiative, showcasing the Commonwealth and its values, increasing public visibility and personalising the Commonwealth connection for millions of individuals. Its website connects audiences and enables professional and expert collaboration on a titanic, trans-world scale.

Then there is the Commonwealth Local Government Association (active at a highly practical level in many countries), the Commonwealth of Learning spreading teaching through open and distance learning (ODL) on a world scale, the Association of Commonwealth Universities (530 of them!) and of course the whole world of sport and the Commonwealth Games administration. The list goes on and on, and grows with all the new professional skills, interests, specialisms and technologies the age produces.

The Commonwealth of Learning, based in Vancouver, is a particularly fascinating example of networking at the most practical level. Supported by 50 Commonwealth governments, it is literally the world's only intergovernmental organisation solely concerned with the promotion and development of distance education and open learning.

All this is usually called 'the Commonwealth family'. what exactly is this vast family? There are 82 bodies listed as accredited organisations with the Commonwealth 'family'. Many more lie outside the official accreditation list. Ranging across almost every conceivable branch of human co-operation, they are the programme material and data for the ultimate global network. Alan Turing, said to be inventor of the computer, would have built a 'thinking machine' to handle them in no time. But his work would not have been necessary. The Commonwealth network machine is busy building itself.

The changing Commonwealth is supported by a battalion of non-governmental organisations, covering a vast range of interests and activities. But in the new age of transparency and accountability worldwide, in which the web and the mobile phone camera open almost every window of activity and social trend, this meshwork of contacts has been given a kind of blood transfusion. In effect, the Commonwealth 'badge' has become a sought-after asset – an entrée to the community of trust, reliability and transparency for which the world's investors and traders constantly search. This is certainly one explanation of the fact that countries with only a remote link with the old British sphere, or none at all, have either already joined the Commonwealth, or aspire to do so, or at least seek to link up with its various supporting groups.

For nations like the United Kingdom, which seemed in past decades to lose interest in its Commonwealth connections, the entire network assumes a new and crucial significance, as the gateway to new markets and new sources of finance – the reversal of the nineteenth-and twentieth-century pattern. Not only have Commonwealth countries become new and demanding consumer marketplaces, ready for the highest-quality goods the UK can turn out. Australia and the Pacific Commonwealth nations lead the way to Chinese markets, via the once-British and still welcoming Hong Kong. Oil-rich Trinidad and Tobago leads the way into Latin America, again mostly with welcoming and Britain-friendly consumer classes.

A flood of figures is beginning to provide more eloquence than words could about the Commonwealth impact on world and British affairs. In the Fraser Institute's Index of Freedom, five Commonwealth nations are in the top ten. In the World Bank's 'ease of doing Business' rankings, seven Commonwealth countries are in the top 25. In the International Corruption Perception Index, seven Commonwealth nations are in the top 25 for being least corrupt.

Commonwealth nations are among the fastest growing, and the momentum is spreading out from the traditionally rich states to the historically poorer ones, particularly in Africa. Trade between the UK and the rest of the Commonwealth (goods and services) has expanded over the last decade by some 150 per cent. Intra-Commonwealth trade and investment flows are also growing fast, although it is hard to extract precise figures. At the Heads of Government meeting in Perth, Australia, in October 2011, a cascade of new investment projects was announced, together with tie-ups between mining interests – for example, between Australia and Nigeria – and a new business forum between the Commonwealth and China.

Are not we lucky, and are not we in the UK absurdly short-sighted and inept in failing to utilize the colossal potential of the Commonwealth connection today and the even greater potential tomorrow?

Family Quarrels

Of course, there must be some realism about the Commonwealth as it is developing today – at least at the official and governmental level. Within any family there are differences, even quarrels at times. That is inevitable. So it is in the Commonwealth family, where not all see eye to eye over either governance issues or world issues. Some are well off, some are not at all well off, and the gap may be widening. With new patterns and doctrines of international behaviour being aired and proclaimed all the time – such as humanitarian intervention, the responsibility to protect, the right to intervene – a constant debate is hardly surprising. Sixteen realms, under the Queen, and 36 (at the time of writing) republics and independent states are hardly likely to agree on everything. But the point is that if there are disputes they are not with 'foreigners', not lost in translation, but between members of the family, all viewing each other as closer than, and subtly different in feel and attitude from, foreign states. Heads of government may clash – the aspect most of interest to the media, of course. But below the surface lies a real Commonwealth network, outside the range of governments and their media camp followers, which continues to knit together across the world as never before.

A second reality is that as the Commonwealth network evolves, not all agree as to how standards should be enforced. That there should be high standards in terms of fundamental values and principles of behaviour and governance, to which all members should aspire to adhere is not in question. That is the distinctive nature of the club, that it requires certain standards to be matched. Not anyone can march through the entry door.

But how those standards should be upheld, policed and even enforced is much more controversial. Responding to the times the Commonwealth leaders have sought, and continue to seek, new methods for ensuring principles are upheld in member states. This is work in progress, work to 'advance the Commonwealth's values', as a recent Report and Recommendations on strengthening the Commonwealth 'brand' put it. It is work that is yielding growing results.

A new Charter of Commonwealth values has now been agreed and validated. Cynics may say that this is not for the first time. There have, after all, been a string of declarations and manifestoes down the years, from the Harare declaration of 1992 (irony of ironies, when one thinks what the Mugabe regime did for human rights there) to the Milbank declaration of 1994, to the Auckland Charter of 1996.

What is the difference this time? The difference is connectivity and information. This is a Charter – a Maxima Carta– that sets standards for an age of almost if not completely total transparency. To say there is no hiding place now for brutal and illiberal rulers and their ways is going too far. Many things can still be hidden, and not just in totalitarian regimes. But the hiding places are now much more limited, and for nations that wish to wear the Commonwealth badge on their lapel far more limited still.

There are miscreants and outliers. Many families have them. Some Commonwealth countries have wanted far more in the way of policing within the club to ensure good behaviour and examine deviations. Other countries have seen this as unwarranted intrusiveness, either because they fear that examination would show too many deficiencies or because they reckon that internal controls, exercised by accountable internal authorities, are best, or because they see an outside inspecting body to be another unnecessary layer, or for a jumble of all these reasons. Whatever the motive, the proposal for an independent Commonwealth-wide Commissioner for Human rights has been rejected as going too far.

Conclusion

'The Commonwealth is in many ways the face of the future.' These were the words of Queen Elizabeth, Head of the Commonwealth, in her Christmas message of 2009. Scarcely attracting the attention of commentators at the time, they are now beginning to be appreciated, a few years on, as what they truly were – namely, a prescient glimpse of the future in a totally transformed international landscape, a beam of light suddenly illuminating a global future which even now may not be fully understood or accepted.

For what today's Commonwealth is developing into is something quite different from the past. It is becoming the necessary network of the 21st century.

Today the UN struggles to reform but remains at loggerheads over its own reform, over fundamental issues and facing severe internal problems to boot. Nothing could replace it but something else seems to be needed in the twenty-first century. The various regional alliances and organizations are growing in power, but by definition lack the global spread the Commonwealth offers. The European Union is the biggest and potentially the most powerful regional bloc but is beset by fearful current problems which hold it back and becalm its economic activity. The WTO spent a decade struggling with deadlock on farm subsidies, while those outside the existing trade blocs feel increasingly frustrated at their still substantially barred access to the richer markets.

By contrast the Commonwealth scene looks somewhat more positive. Intra-Commonwealth trade appears to be expanding steadily, as are investment flows between Commonwealth countries. As a Bloc, the Commonwealth is historically one of the most successful collection of nations in world history. It represents a truly vibrant global family of cultures, economies, societies and stable political groups.

In the age of the internet mesh, in the age of platform business models and blockchains, in the age of totally new trade flows and supply trains, it is becoming daily more obvious where our national assets lie and how they should be used and developed. The Commonwealth is not only offering the fastest growing new markets; it is not only generating investment capital and new skills on a phenomenal scale. It is also the gateway to all the other rising powers of Asia and Africa and Latin America.

CHAPTER FOUR

Twenty Years of Disappointment

Twenty-two years ago, in 1996, the House of Commons Foreign Affairs Committee produced a seminal report on 'The Future Role of the Commonwealth'.

When it appeared this Report was greeted with loud praise because it seemed to be saying something new. Its central and explicit message was that the Commonwealth, far from being past its time, was acquiring a new significance in the modern world by virtue of its unique network qualities. The Report argued that the Commonwealth of yesterday, with its historic connections, had given way to something quite new and not yet fully appreciated. Here we now had not a fading and constantly whinging talking shop but a real and dramatic resource for the future benefit of all its members, especially Britain, and of the whole globe – an organisation not just of history and superficial club congeniality, marked by regular gatherings and photo opportunities, but of real value, passion, purpose and relevance. Strings of recommendations for re-enforcing this new reality were added, some of which have indeed been implemented .

Yet looking back one can only be profoundly disappointed. Somehow the grand new vision has not emerged. Indeed, it could even be argued that the Commonwealth has lost still more of its shine over these last two decades, as it has struggled with the Zimbabwe tragedy and as other great dramas have passed it by. Was the Report therefore, although striking a new note at the time, being insufficiently radical and imaginative? Was it merely trying to build new hopes and new structures on old and weak foundations?

That is what I believe went wrong. The Commonwealth concept of shared values, customs, language and countless exchanges at both governmental and non-governmental levels, remains as valid as ever, or even more so, but the Commonwealth framework needs re-assembling on a somewhat more ambitious scale, to meet entirely new needs, not met elsewhere, in the transformed global conditions now prevailing.

Yesterday, twenty years ago, we still saw the USA as the one dominant and, so we thought, invulnerable superpower. Our hopes for world peace rested, perhaps too heavily, on the United Nations. Yesterday we thought a united Europe could play a kind of bloc role in counter-balancing US might and protecting and projecting its member states' interests and influence.

Now we see that these perceptions were either wrong or too small. The new security challenges are totally global. Issues like terror, energy security, migration, disease control, climatic upheavals and disasters – all demand a world-wide network of approaches. Meanwhile the centre of economic gravity is shifting fast – away from the old West and into Asia, with the three super-giants, a resurgent Japan, China and India at the heart of the new order.

But the shift of circumstances is even more complex and deeper than this. The pattern of international capital flows is beginning to change. Investment which used to flow from West to East, from Europe to Asia, is going into reverse, with Chinese and Indian acquisitions in Europe, for example, mounting . At the same time a 'south-south' stream of investment is building up, with India, South Africa, Malaysia and Singapore all becoming substantial suppliers of capital to other (mainly Commonwealth) developing countries.

An even more powerful, but barely yet understood, development is the supply chain phenomenon which enables producers to disaggregate and outsource crucial segments of the production process, whether services or manufacturing, to lower-cost operations in developing countries.

Being part of the European club may have been useful, but it was not frankly going to help us much in these new conditions. We need something more to keep us connected, refreshed, in touch – and also safe.

The alliances and groupings of the near future, to be economically comprehensive and efficient, need to consist of both advanced and developing countries, to take full advantage of supply chain economics. While it is true that the enlarged European Union has been able to benefit from low-cost operations outsourced to the newer central European member states (amidst many complaints about unfair, low-wage competition), and while it is also true that Western firms are busy outsourcing, despite the political risks, to China, the opportunities are far riskier than, and not half as reassuring and easy to take up as, those offered by the trans-continental Commonwealth network- a structure which entwines economies at virtually every level of the per capita income and wage scale, from the lowest to the richest and highest, in a network of common values, practices and legal procedures.

There is also the question of size. Small countries have proliferated in the last thirty years and, empowered by information technology, seek a more equal voice with the larger nations. In the EU they have been conspicuously denied this , but in the Commonwealth forum it is a different story. There, thirty-two smaller states speak on equal terms, and without being patronised, with twenty or so larger ones, with India as the giant, but a giant, nonetheless, among equals. Promoted by the Commonwealth Secretariat enormous efforts have been taken to understand and assist with the problems of smaller nations in today's world conditions, under the aegis special expert groups – creating an ambience of welcome to smaller states in stark contrast to the big-power dominated EU.

But the most striking 'new' Commonwealth feature of all is the rise of India. In terms of purchasing power parity India is now the world's fourth largest economy. Predictions and extrapolations always need a large pinch of salt, but what they are saying is that India's share of world GNP will rise from 7 percent now to 11 percent by 2025. By 2035 India's GNP with exceed that of Western Europe. Together with America and China, India will form the third 'pole' of the global economy. Currently India is growing at 7 percent, a fraction slower than China (according to official statistics). It has become one of the world's biggest producers and exporters of software.

Of course there are dark sides. One quarter of India's population still lives in abject poverty (it was half in 1978). Regional disparities are vast. But the new overall picture is undeniable. India has become an economic powerhouse. It is indeed the jewel not in the crown but in the Commonwealth. Thus we have a ready-made and intimate network of nations, large and small, rich and poor, developed and developing, all embraced in the same wide web of linkages.

Not only does this put side by side the most dynamic and fastest growing knowledge-based economies – not just India but Australia, New Zealand, Singapore, Malaysia, Canada, Britain itself) – with some of the poorest and most in need of support and friendship. The Commonwealth's official structure also provides a perfect umbrella for a mass of non-governmental affiliations and bonds which give a substance and strength to international relations of a kind which official inter-governmental exchanges cannot provide.

Moreover, modern Commonwealth countries are not only generating capital and output on a vast scale, but also skills. India alone produces 500,000 engineers a year. The advanced technological and engineering skills we in Britain need to prosper are going to be drawn heavily from Commonwealth countries. It is interesting (and regrettable) that our current immigration policy is heading in exactly the opposite direction, making it much harder for skilled workers and technicians to enter Britain from the Commonwealth.

Trade

Today's Commonwealth of 53 nations may contain some of the world's poorest nations but it also embraces a growing number of the fastest-growing and the richest on earth. Trade between them fell spectacularly in the second half of the last century but is now rising fast, as are capital and investment flows, not least because these are countries generating enormous savings looking for a profitable outlet. Intra-Commonwealth trade has been growing at 10 percent per annum since 1995, now above $600 billion and heading for $1 trillion by 2020, and projected to reach $2.75bn by 2030. Indeed some of it is coming our way - and very useful it is as 'inward investment' boosting our home economy and financing our capital projects.

The twenty-first century world is seeing a remarkable reversal of roles. The capital which used to roll from west to east in the last two centuries, from the great industrialised nations to the developing ones, to build their infrastructures, is now flowing the other way. It is the high saving, fast-exporting nations of Asia, in particular, which have the wealth accumulations the West needs to meet its own requirements, square its budgets and update its often dilapidated facilities.

This of course is the opposite of what we read in our nineteenth and twentieth century textbooks about the West pouring capital into the developing nations. Now it is starting to be the other way around. Exports from Britain to the rest of the Commonwealth are now about 10 percent – far below the figure in the post-war heyday when the Commonwealth took almost half Britain's exports, but notably above the even lower figure of recent years and, more to the point, rising fast.

On top of that there is the question of natural resources and the wealth, if carefully managed, that it can bring to previously struggling economies. Revolutionary changes in raw materials potential and access have altered the picture heavily in the Commonwealth's favour. The old resources were oil, coal and iron ore. The new resources are shale gas – accessibly now in vast quantities in Asian and African countries which previously had to import all energy – plus new ways of harnessing sun, wind and the tide, plus precious metals and rare earths hitherto undeveloped or even discovered. Commonwealth countries who were resource poor and are beginning to see themselves as resource rich.

It is increasingly information and services which are going to make up the bulk of international transactions and exchange –and indeed are already doing so. It makes less and less sense nowadays to distinguish between 'manufacturers' and 'services', as the statisticians persist in doing. A telling adage these days (which I think comes from HSBC) is that 'in the future goods will be transmitted rather than exported'. Almost all physical products now have a significant information and service content, whether via actual electronic parts, or via the machines which make them, the design input which shape them, the research behind them, the marketing and sales which transports and distributes them or endless other connections at every point in the production process.

So we can forget the steady moaning about 'declining' British manufacturing, as though metal-bashing was the only virtuous kind of industry. Aero-engines, intricate and incredibly advanced machinery, ultra high tech health equipment, training systems, defence equipment, car components, even simple households goods– it is all one big and compacted bundle of goods and services combined.

In short, modern manufactured products nowadays have become vehicles for exporting knowledge-intensive services, creative items and technology expertise in which the UK has developed an enormous advantage. Typical examples are the whole fields of education and health care. These are so now so large that with all the industrial and research ecosystems they have spawned and carry with them they are beginning to stand alongside the biggest 'service sector 'of all, namely financial services in every shape and form.

And there's more still. By far the most promising markets for our huge services exports are countries with English as the working language and the same or similar systems of commercial law, accountancy and general business practice, in a word - the Commonwealth. By contrast the EU Single market for services barely exists. Always on the verge of being 'completed', so we are told, it remains a forest of obstacles and deterrents.

Since the days in the last century when the original European single market was conceived completely new patterns of international commerce have grown up. These have been described as a spaghetti bowl of regional and neighbourhood trade arrangements. Modern cars (computers on wheels, some call them) may be 'created' in six different places before being finally marketed, making it almost impossible to apply rules of origin (i.e. to say where they were actually made).

Values

Aside from the utterly transformed economic scene, two billion people (31 percent of the world's population) are now linked together in the existing Commonwealth by broadly common legal systems, by countless cultural and sporting links (of which cricket and the Commonwealth Games are the most obvious, by there are many more), by widespread use of British education syllabuses and exams and by a huge network of associations, exchanges and friendships – from the British point of view a treasure house of soft power, influence and opportunity.

What all this means is that the Commonwealth is a ready-made laboratory for the types of coalitions and alliances which are going to work in the twenty-first century. As a channel for promoting the healthiest and most fruitful kinds of relationships between the richer and poorer world, and for poverty reduction and successful development it offers a far better prospect than any other institutions inherited from the past century. Above all, it is an open and voluntary system, excellently adapted to the age of the world-wide web, and requiring no heavy central institutions, or constitutions, or a massive central budget to make it work. On the contrary, the Commonwealth maintains, on the slimmest of resources, a powerful momentum towards higher standards of human rights, towards deeper entrenchment of the rule of law and towards sound governance without the need for any large central bureaucracy or accumulation of powers.

The focus now has to be on strengthening the values which bind us and the potential, both social and economic, for advancement for each and every Commonwealth member, large and small. And remember that in a world of networks, unlike a world of exclusive trade blocs, the interests and welfare of the smallest community or island state, become just as important, and just as influential to the whole system, as the largest.

Security

The new story should not just be about bread and butter matters and new economic opportunities staring the world in the face. The Commonwealth needs to be re-assessed in terms of its real weight in securing world stability, in balancing the dialogue with the U.S. giant, in linking rising Asia and the West, in helping to handle the prickliest of issues such as the Middle East and Iran, in promoting better development links, in bringing small and larger nations, poorer and richer, together on mutually respectful and truly friendly terms and in bridging the faith divides which others seek to exploit and widen.

The mounting horrors of terrorism remind us that a globally connected response is required. NATO membership is vital but not nearly enough. Commonwealth military chiefs and security experts already work quietly but closely together. The South East Asian Five Power Defence Arrangement (FPDA), which includes Britain and four other Commonwealth powers, is just one example. Another is that Britain and Commonwealth countries increasingly train together, exercise together, plan together.

In all these areas the Commonwealth, reformed, reinforced, built upon and enlarged, offers, as the former Indian Industry Minister Mr Kamal Nath, wisely perceives, 'the ideal platform'.

In South-East Asia, I believe that close Commonwealth co-operation, both maritime and military, is going to become of increasing relevance. We may all admire and seek to do business with the massive Chinese economy, but we do not want to see an Asia entirely Chinese dominated. Nor do we necessarily want to see the region grow into a confrontational battle-ground between American super-power ambitions and rising Chinese power — what has been called the Thucydides trap.

That kind of stand-off, full of conflict escalation potential, is inherently unstable and a danger to world order. A better pattern in Asia has to be between the Commonwealth powers of India, Australia, Malaysia, New Zealand, maybe with Japan in alliance, not to challenge but to balance the Chinese titan. Britain can play a supportive role. There is plenty of past experience on which to build.

Of course, there are flaws in this new tapestry. Tension is high again between two Commonwealth members, India and Pakistan. Other countries are lagging badly in good governance, human rights and treatment of women. But at least within the Commonwealth family the pressure is on them night and day.

But despite these problems I see the Commonwealth network of today and tomorrow, and I ask you to see it, not as a fading association bound by memories and history, but as a uniquely relevant and immense network in today's transformed international order —and one to which every member, large and small, should vigorously subscribe and which every member benefits increasingly. It is also a network with which several other countries seek to be associated, and my own view is that they should be welcomed into suitable forms of association, if not full membership, without delay.

That should provide a safer berth for states and communities who do not seek full Commonwealth membership but do want honoured and close friendship with the club and its non-governmental agencies. I have in mind the Republic of Ireland, a number of Middle East and African nations and even the Special Administrative Region of Hong Kong.

In a chaotic and uncertain world, with even the United Nations struggling to bring order, the Commonwealth milieu is the sort of association that more and more countries find valuable and supportive.

It will, of course, inevitably be asked, how can such a disparate and scattered grouping possibly be a force and a weight in these dangerous and contentious areas? Who will take the lead? Where is central control going to be?

To understand the answer to these questions requires the biggest shift of all between the 20th century and the 21st century mindset, a shift which many still find it impossible to make. In the 20th Century the solution had to be in terms of blocs, consolidated organisations, centrally controlled in the name of efficiency, organisational pyramids, perhaps with some delegation, but basically radiating down from a superior and central point.

All this has now been invalidated, not only in business but in governmental affairs and in relations between countries and societies. Thanks to the extraordinary power and pervasiveness of the information revolution we live in an era now not of blocs and pyramid tiers of power and management but of trans-national networks and meshes, both formal and informal.

By accident as much as design the Commonwealth emerges from a controversial past to take a perfect place in this new order of thinking and acting. The fact that the Commonwealth now has no dominant member state, or even a coterie of such states, far from being a weakness is now a strength.

Soft Power

Let us remember that while world free trade is a powerful force for good, (and indeed the key means nowadays of upholding a rules-based order in a troubled world), the key ingredient is trust and it's supporting pillars of common language, common values, standards and above all, respect for the rule of law, all underpinned by close affinities and feelings of fair dealings, friendship and cultural and educational exchange. Nowadays it is called soft power. It is no surprise that China, like many other nations, is investing in soft power of all kinds

When I speak in those terms what am I really describing? The answer is I am describing exactly the nature of the modern Commonwealth network. The Commonwealth has emerged in the digital age in a way which is organic rather than governmental. It is increasingly woven together not so much by governmental linkages and directives but by professions, civil society and interest networks of incredible density and power, all outside the governmental range.

I refer to the networks of scientists, of schools and universities, of creative industries, of parliamentarians, of doctors, of financiers, of farming reformers, veterinary experts, engineers, architects, environmentalists, of women's groups of all kinds and all ages, energy and climate specialists, of judges, of lawyers, small business promoters – the list goes on and on. These are the skills and binding forces which generate trust and attract capital investment, from which trade follows.

Networks grow all the time and connect with other networks all the time. Networks never rest. Networks allow and impel the opening out of links for the United Kingdom through the Commonwealth to the great trading groups in South-East Asia such as Mark Two ASEAN, to the emerging trading groups around the Indian Ocean, to the entirely new networks and clusters forming in Central Asia, in Africa and in Latin America, to the Pacific Alliance, to the Trans-Pacific Partnership, now abandoned by America, and to NAFTA.

Above all I expect to see massive connections grow between Commonwealth networks and the great China networks, clusters and global supply chains now snaking across the world. These are bound to expand with the (BRI) Belt Road initiative and the tying up of Chinese, Central Asian and European markets as never before in history. And of course all this has to move forward with the necessary infrastructure of finance, trade facilitation, insurance and so on.

These connections are already producing new levels and depths of relationships between China the UK and between China and the network of Commonwealth countries.

Hong Kong fits superbly into the new pattern. It becomes what has been described as a super-connector between all the inter-active network connections which are shaping the digital age and transforming international trade and commerce.

This is the new world which leaves the old 20th century centralised European model of integration and protection far behind. Indeed, in this new age I have heard the Commonwealth described as "the mother of all networks". It may not yet be quite that. But through the energy of its peoples, the understanding of its leaders and the unstoppable powers of communications technology that is what it is now destined to become.

Victories are secured nowadays not just by force deployment but by winning the narrative, by using so-called 'soft' as well as hard power methods to safeguard and gain grass roots support for our values, and reject and defeat nihilism and anarchy. For deploying Britain's undeniably immense, but still underused, soft power assets the Commonwealth is the ideal network and platform, even though it has some backsliders.

Foreign Policy & The Power of Identity.

The implications of the Commonwealth are not all on the external side. A nation's stance and standing in the world are directly linked to the cohesion and health of the society within. As Japan's highly successful former leader, Junichiro Koizumi, put it 'Diplomacy is directly linked to internal affairs'.

Pollsters and focus groups strategists tell us that 'foreign policy' is a low category in the list of people's concerns. Education, health, crime control and social policy come far ahead. But this is because they are putting forward 'foreign policy' as a compartmentalised category and therefore asking the wrong question. Most people do not think in these terms. They can see, but may not express, how the nation's status and positioning in the wider world in practice is directly linked to their daily lives, to their jobs, their families' welfare and security, the local environment and countless features which determine their quality of life .

In Britain we seem to forget that in the last few decades, whether by accident or design, the country has become a microcosm of the existing Commonwealth and this should be built upon as an asset in the next stage of Commonwealth development. A Britain with a more clearly articulated Commonwealth role could be a friendlier and more unifying place for millions who are uncertain where their loyalties lie or with what causes they should identify. When disunity is tugging at every edge of British nationhood, the Commonwealth story could pull powerfully the other way, whether against Scottish separatism, alienated cultural and ethnic groups, or rootless younger generations.

Indeed, the 'Commonwealth within' could be a powerful network in an economic sense as well. The deep knowledge about, and contact with, the markets and business networks of almost every Commonwealth market – not just at the big corporate level but even more at the far more intimate (and often more dynamic) personal and family levels – must be a colossal new asset as yet unrecognised.

For everyone there is a need to have a country and to love it, however unfashionable it may have been in recent years to say so. There must for each one of us be a place to stand, a place to grow up. People, like plants, need soil in which to send down their roots. Those who say we can all live nowadays without a country, or content ourselves with trendy notions of the post-modern state and the international community, or even some higher European loyalty, are mistaken. Love of country is not a vague principle but an everyday necessity.

The genius of the Commonwealth is that it reconciles that necessity with the equal necessity for common action, without demanding any blank cheques of supra-national renunciation.

It is the primary duty of a nation's leaders to articulate and refine that idea. This task has now become ten times more important as national security has to be re-defined, as the old power centres melt away, and as the control of so many parts of national life slips into remote hands or the anonymity of the markets vastly empowered by the information revolution.

At the start of this revolution, the more thoughtful and far-sighted could see, and duly predicted, that it would change everything. It has. Above all, it has changed the way we have to defend ourselves, our values, our societies and our environment.

Never was it more important to reject the old generalisations and cliché–ridden simplicities about 'democracy',' freedom', 'our values', 'our way of life' and to unravel the inner meaning of these powerful phrases. Never was it more important to be on guard against the 'Terrible Simplifier' (to use Jacob Burkhardt's graphic concept) who would have us take cover behind stereotype thinking and yesterday's mindsets. Never was it more important for a nation in Britain's position to seek out and work in the right and respectful relationship with the right new partners in the utterly transformed global conditions which have emerged and now prevail.

Our old partners, or so we thought, were across the Atlantic and next door in continental Europe. Our new partners are going to be in East Asia, in near and central Asia and in South-East Asia. These are the regions where tomorrow is being shaped, both economically and strategically. Indeed, are new partners are across the whole web-enabled, levelled planet.

Has the Penny Dropped?

Has the penny dropped? Has the British Establishment, which for a generation has turned its back on the Commonwealth – with the noble exception of the Queen and members of the Royal Family – at last begun to see that it made a terrible mistake?

Have the policy-making grandees of Whitehall and Westminster at last realised that far from being a nostalgia-ridden club of the past the modern Commonwealth network, with its colossal reach across almost a third of the human race, is for Britain a golden asset of the future?

Countries like Canada, India, Australia, New Zealand, Singapore, Malaysia now offer not only some of the wealthiest consumer markets, but also growing sources of international capital, with others like Nigeria, and Sri Lanka, for all their internal troubles, or Mozambique or Ghana coming up fast. And these countries are in turn potential gateways to the biggest rising powers of all, China and Japan, now respectively the second and third largest economies in the world.

Meanwhile, East Asia has suddenly begun to sprout new (or rather revived old) trade routes and activities. China's ambitions for new rail, road and air routes, indeed whole new cities, are moving off the drawing board in the form of a 'New Silk Road' linking Asia and Europe as never before.

To see things through this new lens demands a changed mindset amongst policy makers and the flag-carrying developers of Britain's global business, brand and reputation. We are talking about nothing less than a grand repositioning of the UK in a world utterly transformed by the digital age.

CHAPTER FIVE

Towards a Commonwealth Mark Two

The idea of the Commonwealth as a marginal international institution, doing good works, uttering virtuous aspirations and blessing a host of unofficial organisations is now completely redundant. We face entirely new international conditions and in these the Commonwealth should shed its past diffidence and prepare itself to take a lead in setting the global agenda.

This will require the Commonwealth to raise its game all round, expand its ambitions and activities and forge new links with non-members. It needs to demonstrate boldly its new significance both in the promotion of world trade and investment (building on the role it has already begun to carve out in the WTO debate) and on the wider geo-political stage.

This in turn depends, of course, upon its leading member states. Until they wake up fully and understand the staggering potential of the new Commonwealth network, as an ideal model for international collaboration in the 21st century, the backing needed will not be there. This means persuading Commonwealth Governments to give place and recognition to the Commonwealth network in their foreign and overseas economic and development policies at a level which, for various reasons (mostly now outdated), they have hitherto failed to do, the big exception being India, which almost alone, with its new flair and dynamism, has recognised the Commonwealth as 'the ideal platform for business and trade'.

So, the first task is to bring home to a half-interested world a few new facts about the Commonwealth system which have clearly escaped them.

First, far from being a run-down club, held together by nostalgia and decolonisation fixations, today's Commonwealth now contains thirteen of the world's fastest growing economies, including the most potent emerging markets. Outside the USA and Japan, the key cutting edge countries in information technology and e-commerce are all Commonwealth members. The new 'jewel in the Commonwealth Crown' turns out to be the old jewel, dramatically re-polished and re-set, namely booming India, the world's largest democracy with a population set to exceed China's.

This presents a picture so far removed from the old image of the Commonwealth, bogged down in demands for more aid and arguments about South Africa (or latterly Zimbabwe) that many sleepy policy makers find it simply too difficult to absorb. The unloved ugly duckling organisation has grown almost overnight into a true swan. Or to use a different metaphor the Commonwealth of today and tomorrow has been described as 'The Neglected Colossus'. It should be neglected no longer.

Second, it has been recently estimated that in the new information age context the Commonwealth's commonalities of language, law, accounting systems and business regulations gives a 15 percent cost advantage over dealing with countries outside the Commonwealth.

As for finance, the market capitalizations of Toronto, Sydney and London alone, combined, exceed New York's. The assets of the financial services sectors of the Commonwealth group of nations are actually now larger than those of the whole EU.

Thirdly, on the economic and commercial front it should be noted that recent detailed academic analysis has identified a growing 'Commonwealth effect' – namely a perceived reduction in what is termed the psychic distance between Commonwealth member state, and a consequent increased propensity for Commonwealth states, especially the smaller developing ones, to engage in increased trade and investment activity between each other in preference to, and prior to, trade and investment elsewhere in the global community.

Expansion & Inclusion

Today's Commonwealth has precisely the kind of spread needed for the conditions of the 21st century. But the trouble is that it is not nearly wide enough, nor confident enough to use its weight and authority. The rigid requirement that membership demanded some previous association with the British empire has long been relaxed. Mozambique, Rwanda and the Cameroons are now enthusiastic Commonwealth members. Others are knocking at the door or seeking to associate themselves with some of the pillar organisations at non-state level.

English is already the language of the information age, the necessary universal second tongue. Actually first languages are getting more diverse, and that is welcome. America speaks almost as much Spanish as English. Old dialects and their cultures are being vigorously revived or preserved. Within the UK over 300 languages are regularly spoken and the Metropolitan Police alone prepare advice on emergencies in over one hundred languages.

So the English speaking world now means everything and nothing. The best approach is therefore to think in terms of bringing into this network of common wealth and interest all the nations interested in associating with Commonwealth values and objectives and which really are going to dedicate themselves in earnest or protect and promoting our common interests, security and democratic inclinations. That should be the focus of a truly contemporary British foreign policy.

It may be asked which countries should it leave out? The exclusions should be the vendetta countries, the ones that hate America on principle, hate the advanced world on principle, are still submerged in anti-colonial bitterness and prejudice, do not really care a jot about poverty reduction or the place of women or the dispossessed and do not want to join or strengthen the international system of trade and security.

The new inclusions should be the nations who have shed all this baggage, who see trade, entrepreneurialism and innovation as their guiding stars, who have no time for protectionist blocs and practices, who do not believe (as too many regrettably still do) that development is all a question of bigger aid donations, and who are prepared to do their full bit to preserve peace and resolve conflicts in a way the UN seems incapable of doing .

If it is asked whether there is room for accommodating more than one monarch in this expanded Commonwealth of nations the answer is that we already have this situation and of course it can be arranged and expanded warmly and gracefully .

So the injunction to the Commonwealth leaders should be to open their books and minds to like-minded and powerful countries, large and small, which broadly share these ideas and approaches. If outright membership seems too radical then there could easily be some looser form of association.

One obvious candidate for this kind of relationship is Japan, a nation reviving economically, democratic, increasingly dedicated to helping world stability and peace, committed to open trade, albeit with a few shortcomings (but then we all have those) and seeking a relationship with the US which is supportive without being compliant or subservient – just what the world needs.

The greater Commonwealth of the future should not stop there. Of course it already includes the fast awakening colossus, India, as well as several of the world's fastest growing and most advanced and knowledge-driven economies, such as Australia, New Zealand, Singapore and Malaysia. Thailand could be invited into the association network and we would need to add some good European members, too. Poland and Norway would be obvious and welcome members of the team. Nor should some Latin-American candidates be overlooked in due course.

At the other end of the size scale this Commonwealth Mark Two ought to offer a particularly attractive home for many more of the smallest nations in a dangerous world – much more favourable than they are currently finding whether in the EU or at the United Nations . One can only admire the tremendous vigour and courage of states like Slovenia in the Balkans and the amazing Baltic three, including dynamic Estonia which has shown that it is not afraid to set its own path and add its own valuable voice to the international community, rather than be lost in big bloc politics.

In a much looser way the former British connection still exerts some pull. South Sudan has already applied to be a member. The Gulf States, again with historic links, have also shown an interest in being kept in close touch with Commonwealth activity. Well outside the traditional Commonwealth orbit informal voices have been heard in nations as far apart as Algeria, Gabon and Jordan, urging closer links with the Commonwealth. At a more general level, co-operation between the Commonwealth network and the fifty-six member state Francophonie has been discussed and welcomed on both sides, with Canada naturally playing a key bridging role in such a relationship.

Weave this kind of grouping together in a Commonwealth-plus and one begins to have a serious force of real weight, whose opinions would count decisively in the councils of the world. And this would be not just in high-sounding moral terms. Collectively within this grouping there is a vast wealth of peace-keeping experience, as well as of sheer economic power, technological strength and trading weight. Those who say that such a grouping would all be too disparate geographically forget that inside a network it needs only one click on a computer keyboard nowadays to bypass all physical separation and bring allies into the same room .

The Irish dimension

There are other states where serious voices can be heard talking about membership but nothing is said by ministers or at government level. The most interesting country in this category is The Republic of Ireland. The historical baggage here is almost crushing. Ireland declined to join the 1949 Commonwealth, which first admitted republics, although history has it that Eammon de Valera, who could hardly be described as pro- British, oddly wanted to stay in. In any case there would have been an instinctive dislike of any

British-tainted institutions, and the 1949 Commonwealth must have looked to many very much like the old British Commonwealth in new packaging. The situation is temporarily on hold, given the problems of Brexit and the invisible border. But in due course deeper and more positive trends, one hopes, will resume.

Today the picture is somewhat different. First, the Commonwealth of today and tomorrow is no longer such an Anglo-centric entity, whatever its origins and history. Second, although Ireland has admirably recovered from its euro travails (helped by a large British loan) its commercial links both with Britain and outside Europe have grown in importance. Commonwealth membership would not in any sense be an alternative to its firm EU adherence, but two horses can be ridden and insurance against further financial misfortune would be prudent. Third, the Queen's visit of May 2011 proved outstandingly successful in healing old wounds and promoting reconciliation. Fourth, there is a question of mindset. Bringing Ireland and the UK, as fellow members of the Commonwealth, alongside each other in that orbit ought to be an opportunity for reinforcing institutional links. The Council of the isles has long existed, although hardly in a state of public prominence. The new thought, yet to mature fully in either Dublin or London, is that Britain and Ireland need each other as never before. The combined voice of the whole British Isles would carry new weight in an international context. The mutual economic benefits would multiply. New areas of co-operation in everything from cultural creativity to offshore energy possibilities would open out. Inter-island transportation might lend itself to revolutionary technical possibilities. These are the areas to which the first step, membership within the Commonwealth network, might lead.

It will all take time, but there is a growing campaign for this to happen. No allegiance to the Crown is involved and the Commonwealth of today is a very different institution from the one which Ireland walked away from in 1949.

Of course the Brexit situation, with its knock-on effects on North-South relations in Ireland is an obvious complication, diverting all Irish-British efforts for the time being to solving it and sustaining a largely invisible border.

And of course lingering Republican suspicions remain of anything that appears to involve British intrusion. But this would be partnership without dominance in a changed world, and fellow-membership in the worldwide Commonwealth network, opening up links and access opportunities to many other regions. And what a partnership it could be! Value would be added for both countries.

In reality the overlap of interests between Ireland and the Commonwealth already exists and is growing. Some 40 million Irish people live in Commonwealth countries. A changing world landscape may have turned the idea of Ireland's return from a possibility into a probability.

The existence of a queue of interested applicants is itself a kind of message. It does not, of course, guarantee that they will be admitted. A careful balance has to be struck between the danger of dilution and the invigoration of new members entering the Commonwealth family. Either way, the fact that states and societies round the world are privately urging their governments to consider applying, or are actually sending representatives to Commonwealth events, says something. It says that the Commonwealth is today's club of preference, the group that countries ambitious for improvement feel they should join.

The precise status or category of new member states matters not at all. Queen Elizabeth is the ruler, the monarch, quite separately and independently of 16 Commonwealth countries, the so-called realms. The rest are republics or separate kingdoms. New applicants for returning to realm status seem unlikely, although in this modern turn-turtle world of contradictions and reversals, stranger things have happened. Fourteen other British overseas dependent territories nestle in under British membership, but increasingly aspire to have a bigger role at the Commonwealth table.

American 'post primacy'

The might, size and reach of the new grouping, suitably co-ordinated, would give its members the chance to correct the most dismal feature of today's geopolitics, namely the collapse of American soft power throughout almost the entire world. The decline of America's 'soft power', reputation and influence almost across the entire globe, dragging Britain down some of the way with it, is a tragedy.

The failure in Washington thinking (as well as in London and Brussels circles) to understand what has happened, and the sad collapse of America's 'soft power', reputation and influence almost across the entire globe is leaving a dangerous vacuum. A powerful Pentagon study described this as US 'losing its position primacy'. It is a measure of American policy mis-handling that a recent survey of over a hundred states showed that ninety percent of them now put closer ties with China above ties with the United States – to the delight, perhaps even amazement, of Beijing.

Into this vacuum, cautiously, subtly, but steadily are moving not the Europeans, with their slow growth and their inward-looking mentality, but the Chinese – with cash, with investment projects, with trade deals, secured access to oil and gas supplies in an energy hungry world, with military and policing support and with technology. A replay in reverse of the fourteenth century is unfolding, when China retreated in on itself and Europe reached outwards to every corner of the planet. Now it is exactly the other way round. The Chinese have been quick learners about the use of soft power in this new world and about applying the strategy laid down over two thousand years ago by Sun-Tzu of 'winning without war'. If only the neo-con intellectuals had read that!

This is a gap which ought to be filled not by the Chinese dictatorship but by the free democracies of the Commonwealth, from both North and South, banded together by a commitment to freedom under the rule of law and ready to make real and common sacrifices in the interests of a peaceful and stable world and the spread of democratic governance in many different forms.

A strengthened Commonwealth, committed to democratic reform and the rule of law, reaching across continents and faiths, and also with a deep purse, should be able to do better. It should be able both to offer an alternative to China's fortuitous gain in reputation by default and hopefully in due course to give a helping hand in restoring America's battered credibility, although this may also require not merely a refinement of American foreign policy but also a re-opening of the United States mind to international perspectives, from which it has been woefully cut off in recent years. One Commonwealth could speak to another in terms of genuine equality and mutual respect which just do not exist at present.

The Commonwealth possesses the vital attributes for dealing with this new world which the old 20th century institutions so conspicuously lack. It stretches across the faiths, with half a billion Muslim members; it stretches across all the continents, thus by its very existence nullifying the dark analysis of a coming clash of civilisations.

Better still if a more confident Commonwealth now reaches out and makes friendly associations with other like-minded nations, both in Europe and Asia. Japan, with some twelve percent of the entire world's GNP, and with its confidence and dynamism now restored, is ready to make links with the Commonwealth, especially with India and Britain together.

The thread which binds the interests of these three nations together – Japan, India and the UK – is potentially a strong one, presenting us with untold new opportunities. We make a huge mistake in not building more strongly on our links with Japan, especially when it is dealing with its tricky and giant neighbour – a task which the prime minister Shinzo Abe (incidentally very pro-British) is addressing with great skill and firmness.

Make such a more active and strengthened Commonwealth a central platform of the international future and there will then be an enlightened and responsible grouping on the planet, ready to be America's candid friend, but not its lapdog - a serious and respected force, both in economic and trading terms and in terms of upholding security and peace-keeping.

Admittedly, this Commonwealth Mark Two would be a geographically scattered grouping, not the sort of regional alliance our history books used to talk about. But in the age of the internet who cares? As partners they are only one click away from each other. Sit down this big and powerful grouping round the table with America's leaders and one would immediately have a partnership of real equality, frankness and mutual respect, with enough influence and clout as well to restrain America's wobblier impulses.

This would be a league or network of willing nations, races and cultures, able to establish an effective framework for world stability in ways which the soured and discredited EU-US 'partnership' is no longer capable of doing.

Britain's new foreign policy priority should be to build up this new kind of alliance, instead of dreaming about pivots, bridges with Europe and the like. The British remain good Europeans, as they have been all along, having saved Europe from itself more than once. But when it comes to twenty first century strategic linkages and alliances, the time has come to think afresh. We need to build on our connections with rising Asia and we need to construct a partnership with the US that really works.

Gender Equality

I have described the Commonwealth as being not merely relevant but 'necessary' – something like it would have to exist in this deeply troubled and unstable world if it had not already grown from the roots of the past. I have also described it as above governments, above most official global institutions, even above history and past grievances and bitternesses. It is family – the strongest and most lasting, and yet the most self-critical and flexible bonding of all. The age of the internet, of almost total connectivity – between almost every age group, every interest and profession, between schools, universities, professions and causes – has made it so.

Armchair critics and columnists like to point out that when it comes to shared values, and the place of women in particular, the 53-member states of the Commonwealth include many backsliders and many examples of female abuse and deep discrimination.

Well that is true but negative. What the commentators do not say is that the Commonwealth offers a forum and an opportunity to remedy like no other. What the columnists, who like to scratch their heads and focus on negative aspects, and who do not, with noble exceptions, grasp the nature of the modern Commonwealth – what they fail to see is that this is the ideal assemblage for addressing the challenge.

The Commonwealth can deliver the focus, the pressure for grass roots action, which no amount of media sermonizing can do. We, the Commonwealth family, can drill right down to the details – of both abuse and required remedy – like no other body.

We can send the message into schools. We can shape the business opportunities through new forms of funding and enterprise support, we can promote the local democratic systems, we can challenge the laws, we can expose and reject the twisted justifications of custom and culture and tribe. We can push for female labour force participation in ways that exactly match local conditions. We can campaign for dozens of local changes, country by country, which better recognize the place of women in the workplace. We can be the bespoke reformers in dozens of societies, as against the generalist vocalizers who fill the airwaves and the printed columns.

We must emphasise that gender equality is the key to economic growth. A society in which women and girls have full equality of opportunity, equal access to education, to work, to all forms of training and personal development, to all positions in government, business and the professions is a healthy and balanced society. And a healthy and balanced society is one which develops and grows. No other does.

This may not always have been the case in history. But in today's world it certainly is so. An economy and a state in which half the population is set below the other half, in which half the potential workforce is set below the other half, and denied equal status, is bound to stagnate and retreat. It is a sick society. It cannot go forwards. It cannot prosper. In short, equality is not just a matter of fairness, and not just an ethical and social concern. It is the high road to sustainable economic progress and development.

You may say that we knew this all along. Yet millions of women and girls are still oppressed, abused, forced into marriages, degraded, barred from living a full life. Outright discrimination against women and girls continues – and quite an amount of it in Commonwealth countries.

What are the factors behind this, the walls we have to break down? We know that the opponents of gender equality are ignorant and worse, in places apostles of pure evil – guarantors of continuing poverty and suffering.

But even where discrimination against women is less blatant and less violent we still hear the arguments that custom and culture must be respected. This is outdated nonsense. I attribute some of the blame to the economists and to statistics about women and work – which fail again to depict how real economies now work, or to quantify the real burden women carry, the most important, and yet unpaid, roles they perform.

As I say, this is common knowledge and the subject of copious discussion and proclamation. We have the G20 committing to new efforts, the UN with all its committees, the OECD campaign of recommendations, national and international institutions and movements in profusion, think-tanks galore – all declaring their dedication to women's equality. Yet the abuse continues, tolerated, condoned, ignored.

Today's Commonwealth is one of the world's best pressure groups for gender equality, for youth opportunity, for mutual help and respect between peoples from large nations and small. Sometimes it falters but always the pressure is there.

It is time we used our muscle. The Commonwealth will play a vigorous part in the struggle for gender equality, but within the Commonwealth there are many driving forces. We have within our network, ready to work side by side, all the dynamic organizations large and small, ready to carry forward the agenda on all fronts.

They include the Commonwealth Investment and Enterprise Council, the Commonwealth Local Government Forum, the Commonwealth Education Trust, the Commonwealth of Learning, the Commonwealth Secretariat itself, the Commonwealth Parliamentary Association, the lawyers, the magistrates, the doctors, the teachers, the scientists, and many more, rank upon rank ready to march.

Let them all prosper, all cooperate, all fight as one army. These are the many spearheads of the new international order, the battlegroups that can win against the giant global evils of today.

The degrading and subordination of women is one of the greatest of those evils. And the utter defeat of discrimination against women opens the gateway in countless states to a more prosperous, peaceful and stable future for all.

Energy

An enhanced Commonwealth should also spread its wings on energy issues. At present there is no global forum in which a variety of free nations, rich and poor, but all faced with the same problems of staggeringly high oil prices, all faced with energy security challenges and all faced with the much longer term need to curb carbon emissions and create a greener and cleaner long term environment, can meet together in an informal atmosphere, exchange views and technologies, and develop some common clout in face of OPEC and the other giant producers.

The present energy and climate dialogue between the richer world and the developing nations is not at all healthy or constructive. The biggest developing countries, such as India and China, have remained predictably cool towards the idea they should now slow down their growth and use more expensive energy to compensate for all the carbon the already industrialised world has already dumped in the atmosphere.

India, China and America have half the world's coal reserves and they intend to burn them. Yet as the former Indian Environment Minister said 'We are developing countries. We cannot give any promise, any commitment to reduce

118

further our carbon emissions'. The Commonwealth might be the forum – and no other exists – where these difficult divergences might begin to be reconciled.

Migration

People everywhere are on the move as never before. The Commonwealth collectively needs to take a creative lead in addressing the consequent fast-growing pressures. This is not just a one-way matter of British entry conditions and visa requirements. And no-one is seeking entirely free movement of labour (of the kind to which the EU is said to be fundamentally committed but which in practice has been abandoned under current pressures), nor for the British open-door approach of the 1950s which did so much damage to immigration policy and prepared the way for today's antagonisms.

As intra-Commonwealth business expands, and intra-Commonwealth cultural and professional ties multiply, the need for easier intra-Commonwealth travel increases. It ought to be possible to replicate something like the business travel card system operating between six members of the Asia-Pacific Economic Cooperation group (APEC).

Britain should be proposing a raft of improved conditions for trans- and intra- Commonwealth movement and travel. These should include a new regime of Business Visas throughout Commonwealth countries, easing of restriction on post-graduate employment, fewer bars to incoming bona fide students, incentives for British students to attend Commonwealth universities. Post-EU the whole pattern of British port and airport reception and classification will also need re-design more in favour of Commonwealth citizens.

It is quite deplorable that in our attitude to students from India we have deliberately discriminated in a hostile way, halving the number of Indian students in Britain, seeing them diverted to America and to Germany and making life as difficult as possible for many newcomers and visitors from India. That is not the right basis of trust and of course no satisfactory expansion of trade will be built without that trust. Our actions harm ourselves, harm our brilliant universities and harm the Commonwealth.

A World of International Organisations

While being part of the biggest European club, the EU, may have been useful it is not going to help us much in these new conditions. The difficulty is one of history. The EU is designed on traditional twentieth century lines of central institutional control and a hierarchy of powers (or competencies). It was created in an entirely different world from the one that is now emerging. In the words of one of the star columnists of the Financial Times, hardly a Euro-sceptic organ, the EU has become 'the wrong institutional platform to deal with globalisation' . We need something more to keep us connected, refreshed, in touch – and also safe.

Europe and the EU, in its 20th century structure, have been shaken to the core by waves of crises. Immigration on an unimaginable scale, severe currency disruption with more to come shortly, extremist politics, over-centralisation and regulation, low growth, high unemployment, the need, only half understood, to adapt radically to new world markets and the new digital age – all beg for a new approach.

NATO may look after Europe, but there is an increasing need to safeguard new global routes and patterns, both physical trade routes and cyber routes as well. Closer security and armed forces co-operation through the Commonwealth network, stretching from the Pacific, across the Atlantic and round the globe again, can provide the ideal support frame for the new security and lifeline protection arrangements required.

In the end the Commonwealth will succeed or wither away as a multilateral forum, depending on its practical usefulness and the clear benefits it brings to its members, very much including Britain. Today the UN struggles to reform but remains at loggerheads over its own reform, over fundamental issues and facing severe internal problems to boot. Nothing could replace it, but something else seems to be needed in the twenty-first century. The various regional alliances and organisations are growing in power, but by definition lack the global spread the Commonwealth offers. The European Union is the biggest and potentially the most powerful regional bloc but is beset by fearful current problems which hold it back and becalm its economic activity. The WTO spent a decade struggling with deadlock on farm subsidies, while those outside the existing trade blocs feel increasingly frustrated at their still substantially barred access to the richer markets. By contrast, the Commonwealth scene looks somewhat more positive. Intra-Commonwealth trade appears to be expanding steadily, as are investment flows between its countries. A recent research paper by the Royal Commonwealth Society showed that the importance of Commonwealth members to each other in trade matters had grown substantially over the last two decades, with intra-Commonwealth exports up by a third. Ranging over issues from competitiveness to gender questions, to human development to environmental performance, the paper found the evidence 'seemed to suggest' that Commonwealth membership brought measurable trade advantage'.

Much more work remains to be done in establishing the full picture of contemporary Commonwealth exchanges. None of this may amount to the case for anything like a Commonwealth Free Trade Area (an old idea attempted twice in the twentieth century, although in very different conditions). That era is past. But it does suggest a pause for thought as to how in today's very changed trading conditions, this extraordinary network, with a reach stretching right across regions and continents and embracing a third of the world's population, might (if it can be strengthened imaginatively) do a better job than the existing battered international institutions.

In particular it is surely time to think of how a more ambitious Commonwealth of Nations could become a distinct force in both opening up the world economy and uniting the more well-intentioned and responsible countries in facing up to the ugly dangers of the age – such as terrorism, pariah nations, entrenched and paralysing poverty, protectionism, inter-ethnic wars, corruption and rotten governance.

What the Commonwealth requires now is perhaps less intergovernmental grandeur and more practicality. What governments need to do, the British government included, is to study more closely, and then reinforce, the strong developments now taking place within the Commonwealth network.

Conclusion

In summary we first reform, enlarge and strengthen the Commonwealth, broadening the very concepts on which it was founded, and THEN, so far as Britain is concerned, we place it confidently at the very heart of our foreign, economic and security policies. I hope that all other member states would do likewise.

This does not make us bad Europeans. Intimate regional cooperation with our European neighbours continues to be required in many vital areas. It does not make us poodles of the USA. On the contrary we would have the opportunity to shape a far more effective voice in dialogue with the Americans than the EU has come near to achieving. It does not make us neglectful of the UN. But the worst disservice that can be done to the UN, reformed or unreformed, is to expect and demand of it the purpose and unity which it can never, by its nature, deliver.

Finally, it does not make us compulsive builders of new international institutions in a world already overburdened by such bodies, some of them far less accountable than they should be. On the contrary, given the tools of the information age only the lightest structure of bureaucratic co-ordination is necessary to achieve rapid co-ordination and coherence.

A Mark Two Commonwealth is not the complete answer. But it could do better than anything forthcoming from the dated twentieth century institutions we have inherited. It would also be a golden chance for Britain to make her full contribution, in a way which our feeble current foreign policy just does not permit.

So let us start moving towards a Commonwealth that can realise all those hopes of our Report two decade ago and which can have the happy side-effect of giving Britain, the originating member, a new and effective foreign policy with real edge, in turn giving the inner nation and society the purpose and cohesion which it at present so demonstrably lacks.

CHAPTER SIX

The Next Step: A Fresh Foreign Policy for Britain

The implications of all this for British foreign policy strategy are profound, positive and exciting. Thanks to the British public, we now must abandon the misguided belief that our foreign policy can be conducted, or our interests protected and promoted, through our EU partners collectively. Their aims are not ours, their weight in the world is not sufficient and their relations with the US are hopelessly compromised. Besides, key world trade and investment issues are now truly globalised and best handled through the WTO forum rather than through Brussels or Washington, or raucous exchanges between the two . The new greater Commonwealth described here would carry a far bigger, and probably more unified, voice in world trade negotiations than the EU.

In the swirl of post-Brexit debate the role of, and the implications for, the Commonwealth have been raised with increasing frequency.

One question is whether the Commonwealth network of 53 nations, with its growing markets and trans-continental spread, could in any way be for the UK a substitute for EU single market membership.

A second question is how EU withdrawal by the UK impacts upon various Commonwealth countries, bearing in mind the strong pre-referendum message from many Commonwealth leaders that the UK should remain and not leave.

This stance is of course in striking contrast with Commonwealth views back in 1972 which were understandably hostile to British EU (then EEC) membership – evidence of how radically world trade conditions have changed in the intervening decades.

In one sense posing the first question is to confuse apples and oranges on a grand scale. The two bodies, Commonwealth and European Union, are of course totally different – in character, origin, structure and relevance to the UK economy.

While the EU is a political construct the Commonwealth is much more organic. While the EU is a mixture of supranational tendencies and intergovernmental cooperation, today's Commonwealth draws its strength from the extraordinary connectivity at countless non-governmental levels, including flourishing business and professional links, which a common working language, common legal procedures, common accounting and commercial practices, and common cultural links both allows and reinforces.

What has emerged in the modern Commonwealth network is not an old-style trading bloc but something much more novel and suited to the network age – a grass-roots-driven type of organisation. Perhaps surprisingly to some, this is proving more suitable to the expansion of trade and commerce in the digital age, with its growing emphasis on information and data exchange, than the more dated EU hierarchy, with its heavy and top-down bias towards centralisation, scale and integration. Thus, the assumptions of 1972 – that the UK's 'destiny' and best trade prospects lay in Europe and not in the Commonwealth, are being turned on their head.

For example, according to a recent report, published by the Commonwealth Secretariat, Commonwealth trade and investment flows of all kinds are now growing noticeably faster than overall world trends, and now account for some 15 percent of total world exports. The report also found a 'Commonwealth Advantage' of up to 20% which is described as the practical economic value, in both trading and investment interchanges, of a shared language and systems between members when compared to non-Commonwealth nations.

UK exports to Commonwealth states, once, half a century ago, 50 percent of the total, have over the years fallen to a low point of about 10 to 12 percent. But from here the upward direction of travel is clear. Whatever relationship the UK ends up agreeing with the EU Single Market the time for a sharply increased focus on both Commonwealth and adjacent markets is now ripe, and crucial for the UK's continuing prosperity, and because of connectivity, for other European economies as well. The EU referendum result means the UK will regain control over its trade and investment agreements once the EU deal is signed. A number of Commonwealth nations have expressed interest in trade talks such as India, Australia and New Zealand. Both Australia and New Zealand have offered trade negotiators to help the UK.

However, the UK must see any trade deals from Commonwealth perspective as well. It must avoid sounding narrowly Anglo-centric. Successful trade and investment relations should be a partnership of equals. Further deals must also cover non-economic relations, including in many cases security. Having shown other Commonwealth members the door back in 1972, we now need to knock politely and ask to be let back in.

When we do so we will find ourselves entering a very different world from the one we turned our backs on all those years ago. Then it seemed that all the best growth opportunities lay in Europe. Now it is to Asia, Africa and Latin America we need to look for the big prizes, and the Commonwealth network is the gateway to many of these fast-growing new economies.

There has been significant structural departmental change with the Department of International Trade under Dr Liam Fox being set up. This new creation is welcome but two further changes are required. First there needs to be a much stronger and freer standing Commonwealth unit inside the Foreign and Commonwealth Office. Second, the Commonwealth ought to be given a voice at the Brexit negotiating table – or tables. For the UK to respond to the new situation requires a vastly expanded degree of attention to Commonwealth member states, large and small. The legacy of common working language and past friendships can certainly help. But much more will be needed. Relying on unreconstructed old ties with Commonwealth member states will no longer suffice.

Successful business has to cover not just actual deals and contracts but a whole framework of supporting soft power deployment – including everything from cultural and professional links to easier and friendlier travel and visa policies.

As the new Commonwealth Secretary-General, Patricia Scotland, told a parliamentary committee: 'Much, much more energy will now go into enriching the Commonwealth relationship', adding that she saw the need now 'to turbocharge the Commonwealth trade advantage'.

This doesn't mean just piling on more trade missions. It means involving the UK more deeply than ever in the new connected world system, and especially in the immense expansion of Chinese infrastructure connections across Central Asia and right into the heart of Europe. Here the Hong Kong connection, with its substantial UK-friendly bias and past history, can be an invaluable aide.

We live in a world seemingly falling apart yet paradoxically coming together as never before through the staggering power of constant and instant communications. Fragmentation versus super-connectivity – the two contradictory forces prevail simultaneously, bringing bewilderment and confusion to governments and governed alike. For the UK in a post-Brexit world it is high time for more Commonwealth togetherness. The case for a decisive strategy of redirection of trade and investment, both ways, and for the supporting policies, towards Commonwealth and developing country markets was strong long before Brexit and will grow still stronger long after the Brexit dust has settled.

Europe is no longer the world's most prosperous region. It is our duty to build up our links, many of which were so strong in the distant past, with what are becoming the world's most dynamic areas, to which both economic and political power are now flowing – and not just the bigger ones but the smaller nations as well, the struggling poor ones as well as the rapidly industrialising and increasingly high-tech ones.

Of course, the UK must continue to be the best possible local member of our European region in which geography places it – as, incidentally it nearly always has been, shedding more blood than most in the cause of saving Europe from itself and securing its freedoms - although some people forget this.

New Commonwealth, New Realities

David Cameron was right when he called for the UK to think in a completely different way not only about our domestic society but also our external role and direction. In fact the two aspects are closely related.

First we have to adjust to the fact that the new Commonwealth is no longer an Anglo-centric affair, or at least not nearly so much so as in the past. Just as power and wealth have shifted globally away from the West, so also within the Commonwealth system the new centres of influence are going to lie in Asia and its enormous markets.

Second, the promotion and safeguarding of British interests is going to require a new diplomatic agility and nimbleness. The Commonwealth network links us up not just with the big new powers but with numerous smaller nations who want a voice, have a contribution to make and deserve more respect and attention than we have given them in recent years, or they feel they get from other international bodies.

Examples are Trinidad and Tobago - not only an obvious gateway to Latin American markets but like other Commonwealth countries a source of swelling investment funds which we, the British will need to tap to fund our vast infrastructure and energy transition needs. The same goes for Singapore and other ASEAN members, as well as for newcomers to the resource wealth scene such as Papua New Guinea. Add in the sovereign wealth funds of the bigger players, such as India, Australia, Malaysia and it can be seen that the Commonwealth of tomorrow could well become our bank as well as our band of friends.

Third, it is time to become a little less diffident about operating as a Commonwealth caucus and speaking up for Commonwealth interests in the many international institutions to which we belong. France seems to have few inhibitions about advancing Francophonie interests in EU circles and elsewhere. Common Commonwealth goals in reshaping the world trading system, pushing ahead with the faltering Doha round and rebalancing the IMF, for example, not only merit reassertion but could also add to Britain's diplomatic leverage in these and other forums.

Fourth we should start valuing more confidently what we have got, thanks to the Commonwealth legacy – a world-wide pre-eminence in the legal and accountancy professions, an extraordinary web of Commonwealth-branded associations of experts in fields from architecture to zoology, and above all a pattern of educational linkages that not only makes British higher education one of our major exports but also sends a stream of younger Brits out into Commonwealth countries.

In short, the emerging markets, the great new centres of middle class purchasing power across the Indian sub-continent, across central, south east and Pacific Asia, across Africa both north and south, and across Latin America, are where we, the British, have to be, and where luckily we have a great deal of experience and skills from our past history to secure our entry.

Our way in is through diplomacy but also through a mass of trading, cultural, educational, social and scientific connections, and not least through the latticework of links between Commonwealth interests and citizenry already here in Britain and their former homelands – the so-called 'Commonwealth within'.

It is the strengthening of this expanded Commonwealth network which the UK should now make its key foreign policy priority and together with which it should re-build its own foreign policy priorities. It should do so because this route offers by far the best way both for a nation such as ours, with our history and our experience and skills, to make a maximum contribution to meeting the world's many ills and, even more, because it is the best way to promote and protect our own interests world-wide.

When the Asian engineer, trained here, specifies new machinery requirements, we want him to look to Britain. When the dentist re-designs his or her operating room we will supply the most advanced equipment. When accountancy skills or legal skills are needed we want the professionals to look to London and operate by common Commonwealth standards and accreditation patterns.

For the UK these past decades have been the years which the locusts ate. Our competitors, including our quick-footed partners in the EU, have not been nearly so slow to grab the opportunities and embed themselves in this new and lucrative landscape.

Nicholas Boles, a new Conservative MP, in a brilliant phrase, has described the problem for Britain over these wasted past years as being 'not delusions of grandeur but delusions of impotence'. It is time for a more distinctive and confident foreign policy which sustains our prosperity and promotes our values. The Commonwealth is one of the key ways of lifting ourselves out of what seemed in the past like a silo of defeatism. It is the modern route through which we not only secure our interests but also offer our example, setting it, as the Pope observed on his recent visit, "before the two billion members of the Commonwealth and the great family of English-speaking nations throughout the world".

Practical Changes

It is time we woke up to what is happening and subjected Britain's external relations priorities to a major re-alignment. And that is why a symbolic re-christen should now take place. The home of our able and experienced diplomats should be re-labelled the Commonwealth and Foreign Office – the CFO not the FCO. Small changes can signify a lot.

Next, the UK should consider transferring the administration of that part of its overseas development effort which at present goes through the EU from that unhappy channel to the Commonwealth system, and encourage both other Commonwealth members to do likewise and the Secretariat to develop the full capacity to handle this role. This single move would give the Commonwealth huge new prestige and resources, direct our aid efforts far more effectively to poorer Commonwealth member states, who are our closest friends and to whom we owe the strongest duty and greatly strengthen the UK's own prestige and effectiveness in the global development process. The current bias in EU programmes towards the Francophonie states could thereby be usefully corrected.

Another important change is to shift our education system so that our children be taught a greater sense of British and Commonwealth identity. That alone conveys the broader and outward-looking sense of interdependence and duty which is the true message with which young British children should carry in today's world.

Scholarship and study opportunities in all directions need to be fostered and increased. Not just one way towards the UK and not just at govern-mental level. All universities, British and Commonwealth, have a part to play in enlarging the volume of scholarship schemes. A 'Commonwealth Trade and Investment Bank' has been proposed by Indian advocates to boost Commonwealth trade and investment potential. Numerous new Commonwealth initiatives are springing up of their own accord, unheralded and unnoticed by officialdom, such as the Commonwealth Environmental Investment Platform, bringing entrepreneurs throughout the Commonwealth together. There is Commonwealth exchange, the brainchild of two inspired young activists, Tim Hewish and Jim Styles, determined to get at the new facts.

Mr Blair was quite wrong to describe the British as 'reluctant global citizens' as he did in Manchester. We are outward looking by instinct and history. And Gordon Brown was comically wrong in his narrow emphasis on 'Britishness'. The whole secret of British influence in the world, which has been out of all proportion to our small size, has been to rise above nationalistic posturings and think, and teach our children to think, about a wider canvas.

To head out to the 2018 CHOGM with imaginative vigour and enthusiasm promises great benefits for the wider Commonwealth Within the global framework. To fail to take this path can only lead to missed opportunities on a historic scale at a time when every ounce of effort should be going into refreshing old links and building new ties in a world in which almost all preconceptions must now be reset.

To play a part in this, the Commonwealth Secretariat should be encouraged to develop its external wing in a much more powerful way than hitherto, and perhaps have a nominated high official to work with the Secretary General and act as the Commonwealth's High Representative. That will of course mean bigger budgetary contributions from the member states. But make such an emboldened Commonwealth the central platform of the international future and there will then be an enlightened and responsible grouping on the planet, ready to be America's candid friend, but not its lapdog - a serious and respected force, both in economic and trading terms and in terms of upholding security and peace-keeping.

Progress Inside the Commonwealth

The search must be for new grassroots initiatives, especially from the Indian sub-continent and from African societies and culture. At the same time continuous Ministerial and

136

official dialogue and discourse needs to be intensified as communications technology now allows.

The Commonwealth Charter stands but it must not be insistently over-promoted as the instrument of Western values in a post-Western age. Instead there needs to be greater emphasis on the 'golden thread' theme that highlights the linkage between values adherence and trust generation on the one hand and entrepreneurial and innovative investment decisions which are the real drivers of economic advance on the other.

The Commonwealth agenda needs to define more clearly where its efforts can add unique and original value to existing world-wide causes, including economic development. Practical steps to promote gender equality and defeat corruption are two examples.

And the Commonwealth needs to be far more sensitive (especially in trade meetings) to the need for reconciliation between the fundamental energy needs of, say, India or South Africa, or Malaysia, and the low carbon objective. Expensive and complex methods for greening power are of poor advantage to struggling communities who at present have neither water nor electricity. The constant and seemingly insensitive harping by some Commonwealth voices on climate measures regardless of cost is a huge negative for millions of Commonwealth citizens.

The need now is for the Commonwealth Secretariat to be encouraged by its members to grow wings. That is to say, it should develop in a much more powerful way than hitherto, the capability to address global policy issues.

Conclusion

The Commonwealth template stretches over this new scene, bringing a clear and calming prospect of betterment and common purpose. Its roots are old, stretching back into the histories of its original members, but its character today is youthful – in the most literal sense. Half the 2 billion or more citizens of the Commonwealth are under 25. For women, its declared aim is a far better future and a much better gender balance generally.

Over it all presides Queen Elizabeth II, as she has done for 60 years past – an undeniably unifying influence, held in high affection and leading the way to the future with vast experience and skill. The paradoxes are powerful – a monarch guiding the way to a new world order! Succession to the role of head of the Commonwealth is not automatic. When the time comes, the Commonwealth membership will want the right to choose. But there is every reason to suppose that the choice will continue to fall on the occupant of the British throne.

As a bloc, the Commonwealth is historically one of the most successful collections of nations in world history. But of course it is not a bloc in the conventional sense. Its links are electronic, not geographical; they are digitally networked, not hierarchical; they are between peoples and societies and the modules within each social structure. The challenge from the back of the hall, or from the journalists in the front row – who is in charge? – cannot really be answered in the usual terms. The nearest answer would be that the people are in charge, or perhaps it is nearer the mark to say the network is in charge. The Commonwealth is a creation of self-assembly. It is not the United Nations, nor even a pale replica of it. And it is not a regional bloc like the battered European Union. It is an escape from these structures and it leads to territory that these organisations do not reach, and often cannot see. This is its power and its weakness. It is a truly vibrant global family of cultures, economies, societies and political groups, far from perfect but looking in the same direction.

In an age of renewed global dangers and uncertainties, while Governments may differ and nations struggle to maintain coherence, the Commonwealth family continues to knit together as never before. The team between peoples, the partnership, the unifying association of common values and purpose which is the modern Commonwealth, stands out increasingly as a network of hope across the planet.

It proclaims the vitality, and ever-increasing connectedness, of peoples across a third of the planet (with others knocking at the door) who are determined to work together in every field from the defeat of poverty and the stability of governance, to sport and games, to art, music and literature – and all in the best causes of humanity.

An Unfinished Odyssey

Here the trail halts, an odyssey unfinished but with one enduring and central fact standing out just as clearly as it did at the start to some of us 23 years ago. In the age of digital revolution – disrupting, connecting, empowering, challenging – the Commonwealth network has acquired, and is continuing to acquire, momentum, potential and significance on a scale hitherto unimaginable. The transformation continues in a radically changed international landscape now taking shape, driven by immense new forces

Networks are living systems. They connect communities, groups, cells, interests, professions, projects, enterprises, inquiring and creative minds, with a frequency and intensity which has never before existed.

In the Commonwealth case there is the added immense binding power of a common working language, and the DNA within that language, which multiplies network power many times over

This means that we can watch linkages and common endeavour connecting all the time between every Commonwealth country and every conceivable sector – between scientists, doctors, vets, teachers, lawyers, universities, schools, enterprise in all shapes and sizes, designers, authors, military organisations, engineers, administrators, legislators, cities and villages, youth movements, museum experts – the list is endless.

Above all it means that the Commonwealth assumes, or re-assumes, a central place in our nation's overseas priorities and policies; it becomes a vast transmission system in the exercise of soft power.

This may not be what national governments or political leaders planned or intended. Indeed in the British case such an outcome has being actively resisted for decades until very recent times.

But while at government level Commonwealth countries may differ and clash, all the while, beneath the media radar, the network process is continuing and expanding regardless – each new connection sparking not only to fresh initiatives and activity but leading through to further contacts with yet further networks beyond. Thus, on a 'friend of a friend' basis, entrée to the whole global connected system, to the new networks and new institutions of the 21st century, opens up before us.

Positive official and governmental policies obviously assist, but with or without them the networks carry on expanding unceasingly.

Some call this the fourth Industrial Revolution. Some call it the second wave of globalisation. For us here in Britain I call it the hour of the Commonwealth, and it feels good to survey the infinite opportunities for our nation which now spread out before us.

APPENDIX

House of Commons Foreign Affairs Committee

First Report 20th November 1995
CHAPTER X EXTRACT

CONCLUDING OBSERVATIONS

204. Our inquiries and evidence have surprised us. At the outset of our enquiry we were fully aware of the historic and sentimental attachment which constituted Commonwealth relations; but our study has identified opportunities and potential which would make Commonwealth relationships meaningful in a rather different way, while at the same time, building upon the natural affinities of shared language and accord political and cultural beliefs.

205. Our report therefore has a central and explicit conclusion. It is that the Commonwealth is acquiring a new significance in rapidly transforming the world and that United Kingdom policy-makers should bring this major change

to the forefront of their thinking. Our enquiries show that the Commonwealth of yesterday, still a stirring perception here has given way to something quite new and not yet fully appreciated. Far from being a 'club' of countries all too ready to both criticise and make demands on the former imperial power, the Commonwealth is rapidly metamorphosing into a network with quite different interests and ambitions.

206. Our report shows the wide-ranging nature of these changing interests and aspirations. These include extensive changes in political and economic relations. However, no less important is the changed emphasis on promotion of democracy, good governance and human rights, where the Commonwealth is increasingly willing to stand up for the values and objectives it espoused at Harare in 1991.

207. From the United Kingdom's point of view, this transformation of vast potential makes it quite essential that we exploit it with vigour and imagination. If energy is created by shared language in the Concord, cultural attitudes and political beliefs make these opportunities all the more attractive, although it's up to us, and no one else, to make the best of them or let them pass by.

208. The new positioning of the Commonwealth network, and of Britain within that network, is to be seen in the context of growing Asian importance, both economic and now in political terms, in the world scene. The recent Asia-Europe summit in Bangkok, where Asian and European leaders were not arguing over demands on the developing world, still less going back to recriminations over past wrongs but instead

were there to discuss on equal terms the ways in which the powerful economies of the two regions could co-operate and reinforce each other, was a reminder of this new context.

209. This is precisely the sort of occasion-and there will be more of them - when this country's unique links with many of the other nations involved through the Commonwealth connection, can be deployed to considerable advantage. We would have liked to have heard more from the policymakers about the emerging possibilities in this respect.

210. However, in our enquiry we were not enormously encouraged that such new ideas had yet taken hold. We were struck by the cautious and downbeat FCO memorandum on the whole subject, although in their evidence Ministers undoubtedly sounded a more positive note.

211. We note that Lady Chalker refuted any suggestion that the 'C' in FCO represented a Cinderella within the department. 339 that is welcome; but our own conclusions in the report now lead us to recommend something much stronger still, namely a whole new strategy to reinforce bilateral Commonwealth ties, to sustain the overall Commonwealth organisation and to deploy the advantages which Commonwealth membership gives us far more systematically, both in diplomatic endeavours and in the furtherance of this country's world-wide commercial interests.

212. We do not wish to impose more administrative structures or overheads on the Commonwealth system. But we believe that within our own national administration, and

certainly the FCO, more minds should be focussed on our Commonwealth role.

The Importance of the Commonwealth dimension does not appear always to be reflected fully in government policy. Decisions seem to be taken on what appear to be perfectly sound grounds, but account necessarily being taken of the Commonwealth dimension, or regard to the way they will be perceived in the Commonwealth. Examples include:

i)   reporting the outcome of CHOGM to Parliament by the way of written answer rather than an oral statement;

ii)   the absence of any reference to the Commonwealth institution in the new mission statement of the FCO diplomatic Wing when any of its 17 long-term aims and objectives and

iii)   the removal (under the guise of a removing anomalies remaining after bringing United Kingdom law into line with European Community requirements) from 1 June 1996 Of the right of Commonwealth citizens to apply for posts in the United Kingdom Civil Service which constitute "employment in the public service" within the meaning of the European Community treaties.

213. A larger more pro-active role for the FCO's Commonwealth Co-ordination Division – presently a seven-person operation – is essential

214. We also wish to see a stronger emphasis on the Commonwealth dimension across the Government as a whole. In hard practical terms, this means:

i)   greater readiness to speak up for the interests of our Commonwealth friends in the various forums of the world to which the United Kingdom belongs, as well as a greater readiness to remind our Commonwealth fellow members speak up for ours - for instance in the Asia-Pacific Economic Forum structure and in ASEAN;

ii)   giving a new governmental attention to the educational and cultural interchanges which used to characterise the Commonwealth and which must not be allowed to languish. On the contrary, they should be fostered more energetically than ever; and

iii)   recognising in shaping our industrial and trade policies, that growing interests and opportunities for British business now lie in the emerging markets of the world, of which several happen to be Commonwealth members.

214. We have heard often in our enquiry, and we do not tire of repeating in our report, that Britain's Commonwealth connections and the integration the global network of communications and friendships which go with the, are the envy of our trading competitors. Surprise is expressed that this country has not utilised them to greater advantage.

215. Perhaps it was understandable for a few decades after the end of the Empire that the Commonwealth was seen in the United Kingdom as a relic of an imperial past - a political albatross around the country's neck. Trauma and uncomfortable adjustment were inevitable, although they should never be forgotten that the unwinding of that

was achieved, the most part, in a relatively peaceful and constructive way.

216. But that era is over, and so is its successor phase of 'decolonisation'. A new global pattern opens out in which the competition to maintain, let alone advance, living standards will be more intense than ever. In this new situation, the United Kingdom has both friends and opportunities. They should be recognised and seized.

Index

A

Abe, Prime Minister Shinzo, 113
Afghanistan, 28
Africa, 41, 54, 64, 67–68, 79, 95
American 'post primacy,' 110–114
America's 'soft power,' 110–111
ASEAN - Mark Two, 95
Asia-Pacific Economic
   Cooperation group (APEC),
   119
Asia-Pacific Economic Forum, 147
Assad, President Bashar, 27
Association of Southeast Asian
   Nations (ASEAN), 62–63, 95,
   131, 147
Auckland Charter of (1996), 77
Australia, 75, 85, 100, 128, 131

B

Belt and Road Initiative (BRI), 95
Blair, Prime Minister Tony, 44,
   47–48, 135
Boles, Nicholas, 133
Brexit, 17, 54, 129
British empire, 18, 104
British foreign policy, 13, 44–45
Brown, Gordon, 135
Bush, President, 26

C

Cabinet Office Unit, 15

Cameron, Prime Minister David,
   53, 131
Canada, 85, 100, 107
Capitalism, 32–33, 37
Castells, Manuel, 37
Chalker, Lady, 145
China, 31, 54, 75, 92, 94, 129
Churchill, Prime Minister
   Winston, 47
Churchill, Sarah, 71
Climate measures, 137
Cold War, 47
Common Foreign and Security
   Policy (CFSP), 45–46
Commonwealth
   agenda, 137
   behaviour and governance, 76
   co-operation and networking,
   59
   Co-ordination Division, 146
   e-commerce, 60
   EU, 126
   identities, 61, 135
   information technology, 60
   international relations, 62
   membership, 122
   neglect, 64
   network age, 67
   networks, 42, 140
   non-governmental levels, 126
   power and weakness, 139
   practical changes, 134
   rigid bloc alliances, 61
   Secretary Generals, 71

smaller states, 68
trade and investment, 127
transformation, 140, 144
Commonwealth 'badge,' 70, 73
Commonwealth Charter, 137
Commonwealth Education
 Ministers, 15
Commonwealth Education Trust,
 117
Commonwealth Enterprise and
 Investment Forum, 72
Commonwealth Free Trade Area,
 122
Commonwealth Investment and
 Enterprise Council, 117
Commonwealth Local
 Government Association, 72
Commonwealth Local
 Government Forum, 117
Commonwealth of Learning,
 72–73, 117
Commonwealth Parliamentary
 Association, 71–72, 117
Commonwealth Secretariat, 84,
 117, 127, 136–137
Commonwealth Summit, 55
Commonwealth Trade and
 Investment Bank, 135
Connectivity, 29
Contemporary Commonwealth
 exchanges, 122
Control and governance, 66
Cook, Robin, 14

D

Decolonisation, 60, 102, 148

Democracy, 27, 144
de Valera, Eammon, 107
Discrimination against women,
 114, 116, 118

E

East Asia, 100
Easternisation, 33–36
Economic growth, 65
Economic policy, 56
Elizabeth II, Queen, 78, 110, 138
Emerging markets, 102
'Empire 2.0', 56
Energy, 118–119
English, 22–23, 104
EU foreign policy, 44–45
European club, 83
European Union (EU), 15, 84,
 120–121
EU-US 'partnership', 113
'Existing nuclear powers,' 31

F

Fanaticism, 51
Financial services sectors, 103
Foreign and Commonwealth
 Office (FCO), 45, 62
Foreign policy, 30, 96–98, 114
Foreign policy priority, 18, 53,
 114, 133
Fox, Dr Liam, 128
FPDA (South East Asian Five
 Power Defence Arrangement),
 91
Fragmentation vs. super-

connectivity, 22, 130
France, 40, 132
Fraser Institute's Index of
    Freedom, 74
Free Trade Agreements, 55
Friedman, Thomas, 37–38, 61

G

Gender equality, 114–118
Germany, 38–39, 120
Global communication and
    connection, 69–70
Global economy, 85
Good governance, 69, 144
Grass roots action, 115

H

Harare Commonwealth
    Declaration (1992), 77
Hard power methods, 96
Hewish, Tim, 135
Hong Kong, 33, 66, 74, 93, 96,
    129
Human rights, 144

I

Immigration policy, 86
India, 31, 83, 85, 100, 106, 112,
    128, 131
Inter-active network connections,
    96
International Corruption
    Perception Index, 74
International relations, 51, 60, 62

Intra-Commonwealth cultural and
    professional, 119
Intra-Commonwealth trade, 78
Intra-Commonwealth travel, 119
Investment, 83
Iran, 91
Iraq war, 26
Ireland, 108–109
Ireland, Republic of, 107
Irish dimension
    Brexit problems, 108
    de Valera, Eammon, 107
    inter-island transportation, 109
    mutual economic benefits, 108
    realms, 110
Israel-Palestine conflict, 28

J

Japan, 31, 40, 51, 60, 92, 100,
    102, 105, 113
JACIKS (Japan, ASEAN, China,
    India and Korea), 32

K

Knowledge-based economies, 85,
    106
Koizumi, Prime Minister
    Junichiro, 97

L

Latin America, 54, 74, 79, 95,
    106, 128, 131–132
Lee, Chung Min, 32
London, 43, 45, 54, 62, 103, 133

Luttwak, Edward, 33

M

Macmillan, Prime Minister Harold, 47
Malaysia, 32, 83, 85, 92, 100, 106, 131
Marlborough, 71
Meyer, Sir Christopher, 48
Middle East, 26–27, 39, 46, 91, 93
Migration, 119–120
Milbank declaration (1994), 77
Modern Commonwealth, 115
Mogherini, EU's Foreign Minister Federica, 45, 49
Multinational organisations, 69

N

Nath, Kamal, 91
Neglected Colossus, 52, 103
Network and cluster concept, 65–66
Networks of scientists, 95
New Silk Road, 100
New Zealand, 40, 85, 92, 100, 106, 128
Nigeria, 75, 100
North American Free Trade Agreement (NAFTA), 95
North Atlantic Treaty Organization (NATO), 121
membership, 91
North Korea, 31
Nuclear power station, 39

O

Organisation for Economic Co-operation and Development (OECD) campaign, 117
Osborne, George, 54

P

Pax Americana, 47
Pax Europa, 47
Policy-makers, 63, 143, 145
Pope, 134
Poverty, 39, 85, 90, 105, 116, 139
Prestowitz, Clyde, 32

S

Scotland, Patricia, 129
Scottish separatism, 97
Security, 91–94
Shared values, 82
Singapore, 32, 83, 85, 100, 106, 131
Soft power, 94–96, 111
Solana, EU's Foreign Minister Javier, 45, 49
South Africa, 52, 83, 102, 137
South-East Asia, 39, 91, 95, 99
Strengthened Commonwealth, 112–113
Styles, Jim, 135
Sun-Tzu of 'winning without war,' 111
Super-global and super-local, 35
Supply chains, 23, 34–35, 37, 84, 95

T

Tariffs, 24
Terrible Simplifier, 99
Terrorism, 39, 91
Trade
   digitalised information, 23
   flag, 25
   inward investment, 86
   manufacturers and services, 88
   natural resources, 87
   revolutionary changes, 87
   single markets, 24
   tariffs, 24
Trans-Atlantic relationship, 46
Trans-Pacific Partnership, 95
Transparency and accountability,
   70, 73
Trilateral Commission, 32
Trinidad and Tobago, 131
Trump, President Donald, 27
Turing, Alan, 73

U

United Kingdom (UK), 18–19,
   31, 38, 46, 49, 53, 59, 64,
   74–75, 88, 95–96, 100, 104,
   108, 113, 126–131, 133
United Kingdom Civil Service,
   146
United Nations (UN), 29, 46, 78,
   82, 93, 105–106, 117, 121,
   123, 139
United States (US), 28–29,
   32–33, 38, 48–50, 82, 102,
   105, 111–112, 125

V

Values, 89–90
Virtual nations, 65

W

Washington, 48–50
Whitehall, 14, 54–55, 100
World of International
   Organisations, 120–123
World Trade organisation (WTO),
   78, 125
World War II, 21, 28, 47–48

Z

Zimbabwe tragedy, 82